DIVINE HARMONY

DIVINE
HARMONY

SEEKING COMMUNITY
IN A BROKEN WORLD

MARY DOAK

Paulist Press
New York / Mahwah, NJ

Cover image by STILLFX/Shutterstock.com
Cover design by Joe Gallagher
Book design by Lynn Else

Library of Congress Cataloging-in-Publication Data
Names: Doak, Mary, 1961– author.
Title: Divine harmony : living community with God and others / Mary Doak.
Description: New York : Paulist Press, 2017. I Includes bibliographical references.
Identifiers: LCCN 2016035608 (print) I LCCN 2017005783 (ebook) I ISBN 9780809153275 (pbk. : alk. paper) I ISBN 9781587686757 (Ebook)
Subjects: LCSH: Communities—Religious aspects—Christianity. I Catholic Church—Doctrines.
Classification: LCC BV625 .D63 2017 (print) I LCC BV625 (ebook) I DDC 261—dc23
LC record available at https://lccn.loc.gov/2016035608

ISBN 978-0-8091-5327-5 (paperback)
ISBN 978-1-58768-675-7 (e-book)

Published by Paulist Press
997 Macarthur Boulevard
Mahwah, New Jersey 07430

www.paulistpress.com

Printed and bound in the
United States of America

To my parents, Sam and Peggy Doak,
my first and best teachers in the
joys and challenges of caring for others.

I am interested only in helping those who are in thrall to an individualistic, indifferent and self-centred mentality to be freed from those unworthy chains and to attain a way of living and thinking which is more humane, noble and fruitful, and which will bring dignity to their presence on earth.

—Pope Francis, *Evangelii Gaudium*

Teach us how to love each other,
Lift us to the joy divine.

—Henry J. van Dyke

CONTENTS

ACKNOWLEDGMENTS

As is true for any book and especially so for a book exploring the importance of community, this work is deeply informed by more people than I can possibly name. My family (including parents, brothers, sisters, nieces, nephews, and in-laws), friends, and church community have sustained me and taught me all I know about my need for others. My husband, Phil, and daughter, Sarah, have been a constant source of joy, comfort, and support, and I am grateful for their patience with my mental and physical absence when I needed to work.

Gratitude is due especially to Fr. Mark-David Janus, CSP, for the idea of this book, to my institution, the University of San Diego, for the research leave that enabled me to launch this project, and to Christopher Bellitto, the most patient, encouraging, and insightful editor one could hope for.

I am grateful also to the many colleagues at the University of San Diego and at the University of Notre Dame who, in addition to the gift of friendship, have greatly enriched my theological thinking and have been wonderfully supportive companions on the journey, including J. Matthew Ashley; Sarah Azaransky; Susie Paulik Babka; Bahar Davary; Michael Driscoll; Russell Fuller; Daniel Groody, CSC; Aaron Gross; Gustavo Gutiérrez; Jennifer Herdt; Mary Catherine Hilkert; Paul Kollman, CSC; Louis Komjathy; Robert Krieg; Gerard Mannion; Timothy Matovina; Gerald McKenny; Rico Monge; Karma Lekshe Tsomo; Emily Reimer-Barry; Karen Teel; Leshe Tsomo; Randall Zachman; and especially Orlando Espín, whose influence is present throughout this book, well beyond the places where his work is cited.

DIVINE HARMONY

The theological wisdom, wit, companionship, and support of Colleen Carpenter, Anita Houck, Jennifer Jesse, and Elena Procario-Foley have contributed more to my life and work than I can say.

Fr. Virgilio Elizondo (1935–2016) deeply enriched my thought and broadened my perspectives with his pastoral, intellectual, and personal generosity. He is greatly missed.

INTRODUCTION

LOOKING FOR JOY IN ALL THE WRONG PLACES

The great African American preacher and mystic, Howard Thurman, grew up in the racially segregated south in the early twentieth century. Living in the Jim Crow era, Thurman knew firsthand the harsh reality of life in an unjust and cruel society, one that took the lives of African Americans at a whim. Yet he devoted his life to redeeming, rather than escaping, community. Although he experienced racial abuse from society, Thurman committed his life to the creation of healthy and nurturing communities, including founding and pastoring an interracial church in 1944. As he wrote, "From my childhood I have been on the scent of the tie that binds life at a level so deep that the final privacy of the individual would be reinforced rather than threatened."[1]

Could it be, as Thurman so strongly believed, that we are most fully ourselves when we are most tightly bound to other people? That we develop our personal uniqueness best when committed to our communities? Dare we hope, as Thurman did, that despite our long histories of separation, animosity, and oppression, it is still possible to seek reconciliation and true community together?

This is in fact what Christianity, along with other world religions, has long maintained. A healthy spirituality is not one that separates, but one that overcomes divisions and leads to greater unity.

DIVINE HARMONY

True mysticism, as mystics from different times and traditions have testified, is an experience of the oneness that all participate in.

But today, at least in the United States, our search for the good life has taken a decidedly individualistic and materialistic turn, with the relentless marketing of products promising personal happiness. So many pleasures are available, at so little evident cost. Glittering stores abound, with countless items promising to make our lives easier, more comfortable, more interesting, more fun. New technologies guarantee greater connectivity, faster information, and further options for interaction. From every direction, we are encouraged to have and to do "more, quicker, easier!"

Yet despite all this attention to new pleasures, it does not seem that we have found the truly good life. Shopping malls are packed daily, and crowded with even more people on weekends and holidays, yet Americans suffer high rates of depression. We upgrade and update our "smart" phones to access the latest apps, tweeting and posting to stay in touch, yet find ourselves all the lonelier. Along with high suicide rates, the widespread abuse of drugs and alcohol suggests a need to escape from the reality of daily life. Instead of the promised pleasure and delight, many find that their lives are filled with unbearable tedium and pain. As I write this, methamphetamine and heroin use are devastating communities in many parts of the United States.

This evidence suggests that we have failed to achieve the happiness so widely advertised and so actively pursued. Despite our consumption of the latest products, social media, and self-realization techniques, true peace and contentment are rare. It is hard to escape the obvious conclusion: as a society, we are seeking fulfillment from things that do not truly satisfy. Simply put, we are looking for joy in all the wrong places.

Perhaps we should not be surprised that, even as mass consumerism dominates societies around the world, religions are not dying (as so often predicted) but instead continue to attract members. Throughout history, religions have bound people together with a shared sense of values and meaning, and still today many turn to the world's religions for a sense of community and direction.

But is there any reason to believe that the two-thousand-year-old Christian tradition has something to teach a modern society seeking an ever-elusive happiness? After all, Christianity has been the dominant religious tradition in the United States and in Western Europe, and these societies have developed the materialistic individualism so culturally powerful, and so problematic, today. Nor do Christians seem, on the whole, to be any less caught on the consumerist treadmill than the rest of the population. Could it be that Christian faith merely adds a little more ritual and fellowship, along with a bit of supernatural support and moral self-confidence, to lives that otherwise differ little from others in this consumerist society?

Yet maybe the fault lies not in Christianity itself, but in contemporary understandings of it. Perhaps it is difficult to appreciate the true meaning of Christianity, or any other religious tradition, in a culture steeped in the modern narcissism of self-reliant individuals responsible for their own happiness. After all, religion is often treated as a product for personal consumption, an option an individual can choose to add to his or her list of techniques for self-realization. One might see a therapist, do hot yoga, and then add some participation in Christian fellowship to round out one's spiritual development.

Perhaps we have not quite grasped the deep challenge of Christianity. More significantly, perhaps we have not been thoroughly grasped by the beauty—and the breathtaking audacity—of this ancient faith.

Such, at least, is the possibility explored in this book. While there is much to learn from all of the world's religions, the focus here is on Christianity, the religious tradition most familiar—but not necessarily fully appreciated or understood—in the United States today. Exploring the stories, beliefs, and traditions that have informed Christian practice through millennia, one discovers that a fulfilling life is presented as one in community, a life of right relationships with God, with all of humanity, and with the natural world. Instead of being asked merely to add a little charity and prayer to otherwise self-focused lives, we are invited to see ourselves as bound to one another. True peace and joy, Christianity teaches, comes from being reformed in the image of a divine love poured out for others.

Not surprisingly, few people (Christian or non-Christian) live as though they are confident that love is ultimately stronger than the fear that pits us against each other, dividing our world into the destitute focused on survival and the well-off absorbed with maintaining their position. Courage, love, and a tenacious hope are needed if we are to risk living as if peace is a real possibility, as if deep divisions can be reconciled and past oppressions replaced with mutual care rather than with new oppressions.

Throughout the centuries and even today, however, Christian saints—known and unknown—have joyfully lived this hope, spending their lives in loving others and building up the human community rather than increasing their own wealth and prestige. Might the faith that has inspired these saints speak to our own most profound desires and our deepest instincts about what it means to live a truly good life today?

To explore this Christian hope as a real alternative to the dominant, self-centered individualism of contemporary life is the project of this book. The first two chapters will investigate the deep Christian belief that humans are best understood as persons-in-community, as social beings that are also each uniquely sacred. The first chapter challenges the contemporary culture of individualism with an exploration of the traditional Christian claim that persons are inherently social, oriented to self-giving love in community. Following this critique of modern individualism, the next chapter challenges the opposite extreme—an emphasis on community to the point of denying the dignity and rights of the person. While it might seem that contemporary American society at least succeeds in avoiding this communitarian denial of individual significance, the second chapter will call attention to ways in which American "individualism" commonly devalues the very person it supposedly puts at the center of value.

Chapters 3 and 4 will deepen this presentation of Christian faith by exploring central beliefs about salvation and social ethics in relation to this understanding of the person as oriented to society. Chapter 3 seeks to interrupt the dominant emphasis on an individualistic salvation with a return to more traditional understandings of salvation as also social, as restoring life with others in harmony and love within the Triune God. Chapter 4 examines the Protestant social gospel movement and Catholic social thought as significant contributions to our understanding of how we might create more just and loving societies in the world today.

The following three chapters will focus on the specific challenges the current global situation raises for those who seek to live the witness of Christian faith. Chapter 5 considers the task of sustaining community amid global responsibilities, with particular attention to the reality of increased population migrations that are reconfiguring both the communities that lose and the communities that gain people. Chapter 6 extends the consideration of community through time, exploring the doctrine of the communion of saints as a reminder that Christians are bound—and responsible—to the past as well as to the future. Chapter 7 looks specifically at the challenges of a religiously diverse age. What does it mean to live this religious vision of community in a pluralistic world? Can we seek to create societies consistent with a Christian view of persons-in-community without denying the respect for diversity required by the sacrality of the person?

The concluding chapter integrates the contributions of each of the preceding chapters, reflecting on the difference that Christian discipleship ought to make in the world, and especially in the

DIVINE HARMONY

United States, today. Christianity at its best teaches a much needed wisdom about the truly good life as one of personal development through active and loving responsibility for others and for the communities we live in. This faith has much to contribute to reorienting our society toward the common good, as well as to redirecting our personal lives toward true joy.

Chapter 1

CALLED TO COMMUNITY

TALK ABOUT COMMUNITY can be uncomfortable to those steeped in the American culture of individualism. Of course, relationships matter a great deal to most people. A harmonious family, a functional civic life, peaceful international relations, perhaps especially a loving and mutually supportive marriage—all these are deeply appealing goals. Yet Americans also prize their own physical and emotional space, and consider personal freedom precious, well worth protecting. I suspect I am not alone in getting a little nervous at too much talk of community. Like others, I fear the constraints of conformity, and I don't like the idea of being pressured to live according to someone else's definition of the good life.

This discomfort with community is not surprising given the iconic characters and heroes that many of us grew up with and that continue to inform the American imagination. When I was young, there were still quite a few films and television shows celebrating the ruggedly self-reliant cowboy-hero, like the Lone Ranger or the characters played by John Wayne (a favorite of my parents). At the same time, the hippie ideal was also spreading, and it seemed to offer a very different sensibility. While the John Wayne "type" was generally tough, nonexpressive, and a loner, the hippie was gentle, in touch with feelings, and often involved in communes and worker-collectives.

1

DIVINE HARMONY

Despite the obvious contrasts, an underlying similarity reveals the pervasive individualism that runs throughout American culture: both the gentle hippie and the tough cowboy, after all, defined themselves by breaking with established society. These iconic American (and strikingly male) characters rejected a decadent society, striking out on their own to find their authentic selves. Even when their projects of self-creation involved constructing novel forms of community, as in the social experimentation of the 1960s and '70s, these new social arrangements were clearly secondary to the predominant ethos so often heard in those years: "Do your own thing."

The 1980s ushered in yet another cultural ideal: the yuppie who embraced the capitalist system and embodied professional success, wearing Rolex watches and designer brand clothes. Again, the yuppie was as different in style from the hippie as the hippie had been from the cowboy. The yuppie was urban, welcomed corporate life, and celebrated consumer excess, while the hippie had been anti-consumerist, refused the rigid conformity of the corporate world, and at times sought to revive pioneer practices of working the land.

Nevertheless, the individualism remained—the yuppie was supposed to be the author of his or her own success, outstripping others in a highly competitive workplace. Like the ruggedly self-reliant cowboy and the gently self-seeking hippie, the capitalist yuppie was predominantly responsible to and for him/herself alone.

This individualism is deeply rooted in the dominant American culture. Updated versions of heroic—and often renegade—individuals succeeding on their own and against all odds continue to dominate recycled movie plots.

No doubt, the appeal of these icons of individualism is due to the fact that the United States is largely a nation of immigrants and of the descendants of immigrants. Whether they came willingly or under compulsion, the majority of our ancestors left behind their homes, extended families, and established communities. A great deal of self-reliance is needed by such immigrants—past and present, the unwilling no less than the willing—who struggle to survive in new and frequently difficult circumstances. Not surprisingly, the ideal of the autonomous individual, freeing him- or herself from the constraints of a settled community to build a new life, resonates with many of the stories Americans tell about their past.

Yet this ideal of the self-made person is not and has never been the whole story, in America or elsewhere. Humans are social animals, after all, and the people who came to this land as well as those already here recognized that mutual help was often essential to survival Fixation on the image of the heroically self-reliant trail-blazer obscures the fact that First Nations' tribal cultures, Mexican American commitment to family and community, and collaborative pioneer practices of wagon trains and barn raisings (to cite just a few examples) have also been integral to the development of this country.

Indeed, the very project of creating the new nation of the United States was a communal endeavor. The American revolutionaries bound themselves to common action when they rebelled against rule by England, a treasonous act punishable by death. They knew that their survival depended on supporting each other, as we see in a remark attributed to Benjamin Franklin at the signing of the Declaration of Independence: "We must, indeed, all hang together, or most assuredly we shall all hang separately."

Those who wrote the U.S. Constitution were also clear about their dedication to the common good. They intended, as proclaimed in the Constitution's preamble, "to form a more perfect union" that would serve the general welfare and would foster greater justice. In other words, they devised the Constitution as a means of cooperation so that their new country could be governed effectively.

Though often neglected in comparison with the self-reliance of pioneers, this commitment to creating a better community runs throughout U.S. history. Creative social experiments abound in our past, including the covenantal community of the pilgrims that founded Plymouth Colony, the utopian communities of the nineteenth century, and the Civil Rights Movement's ideal of the beloved, inclusive community. However radical the hippie communes of the 1960s may have seemed, and notwithstanding their individualist rhetoric, these communes sprung from a deep American tradition of seeking to create a model society, one in which people could live better, together.

Forgetfulness about this history of community encourages the individualism so widespread in America today. Perhaps we should not be surprised that a recent (2013) study by Stanford psychologists found that the motivation of European Americans decreases considerably when they are asked to focus on common action for the greater good of all, whereas their motivation increases when they think about acting for their own personal good. This study followed earlier studies that had discovered that most European Americans define *good behavior* as acting independently, feeling personally in control, and choosing one's goals for oneself.[1]

But what happens to common life and to social ties when responsibility for the self is the predominant concern? If so many European Americans are resistant to acting together for the common good, surely the quality of our public life—and perhaps of all of our relationships—is in jeopardy. Robert Putnam's 2000 study, *Bowling Alone*, documents a dramatic decrease in social engagement and civic volunteerism in the second half of the twentieth century, a loss of "social capital" that he believes weakens both individual and society.[2]

The reality is that the myth of the self-made individual—now rapidly morphing into the self-pleasing consumer—is not only inaccurate but profoundly dysfunctional. An overemphasis on self-fulfillment neglects the web of relationality to which we owe our lives, leaving us ill equipped to sacrifice for the common good of society, or even—at times—for our families. Believing ourselves to be self-reliant, we ignore our very real interdependence and the mutual care through which we develop as persons. Society becomes comprised of stunted people, each preoccupied with defending him/herself against others.

Surely, it is no cause for wonder, then, that the family is seen as under threat, that community bonds are transient, that U.S. politics is so divisive, and that so many are lonely, unhappy, and addicted to the distractions of shopping, drugs, or electronic devices.

THE BIBLE: COVENANTAL COMMUNITIES

We misunderstand the Bible when we read it as though it shares the contemporary American emphasis on individual relationships with God. To be sure, the Bible is filled with stories of impressive figures who are depicted as having extraordinary knowledge of God's will. Yet the Bible is not focused on these individuals in their uniqueness. Instead, the biblical stories remind us that these great women and men belonged to communities, inherited and revised community traditions, and envisioned new patterns of community life based on their understanding of God.

This attention to community is especially evident in the great Exodus story of the freeing of the Hebrew people from slavery in Egypt, the story central to Jewish identity and commemorated annually in the Jewish celebration of Passover. As recounted in the Hebrew Bible, God "remembers" the covenant God has with the descendants of Abraham, and sends Moses to lead the oppressed Hebrew people to freedom in a new country. As they wander in the desert after being liberated, they are offered a further covenant, the Mosaic covenant, with laws clarifying their responsibilities to God and to each other. These laws are supposed to order their life together in the new land, determining the kind of people they will be.

Christians often focus on the first ten general laws, or "commandments," of what is in fact a lengthy and complex set of laws extending through several books. This legal code includes detailed prescriptions about how the people are to live as a community in which they honor God above all (rejecting other gods), establish justice among themselves (including providing for, rather than taking advantage of, the vulnerable), and exercise stewardship in their use of the natural world (refraining from abusing their land or animals).

The students in my university courses are often surprised to discover how specific and even mundane the laws included in this code are. They understand the Bible to be a religious text, and they do not consider the detailed rules necessary to organize life in society to be religious matters. Why, they often ask (with more than a hint of disapproval), would God be bothered about the penalty for someone whose ox has gored another person?

What these students do not initially understand, besides the role of oxen in ancient agrarian societies, is that the Bible is very much concerned with society and with its organization toward greater peace, justice, and human flourishing. The quality of human relationships is a profoundly biblical concern, and the rules that govern a society are, from a biblical perspective, significant religious matters—even when those rules involve tedious considerations and can at best only approximate true justice. As is evident in the laws that run through the books of Exodus, Leviticus, Numbers, and Deuteronomy, the Hebrew Bible is not focused on how an individual might please God on his or her own. Instead, the Bible is concerned with how people can flourish together in society, with life-giving relationships instead of the deadly practices of oppression and slavery they had known in Egypt.

If we recall the story of the first sin in chapter 3 of the Book of Genesis, we find further indication of the divine intention for harmony in community. Adam and Eve begin life in wonderful peace in the Garden of Eden, apparently in harmony with each other, with God, and with the rest of creation. But when the couple refuses the established limits and eats the forbidden fruit, their disobedience results in broken relationships and profound disharmony. They hide from God, blame each other, and are sent from the idyllic Eden into a world of struggle, disease, and death. Instead of the peace and harmony God intended, conflict and disharmony now prevail.

The Mosaic covenant is part of God's plan to restore the relationships that sin has broken. The laws are to guide them *as a society* toward greater harmony with God, with each other, and with the natural world. The Jewish people understand that they are given the mission of *tikkun olam* ("repairing the world"), a mission they fulfill by living as a people who acknowledge the sovereignty of God, seek peace and justice in their society, and care for land and animals. This is no private religious devotion, but a faith that binds people together to witness, as a community, to God's plan for a peaceful world of harmonious relationships.

Turning to the New Testament, we see that Jesus also focuses his ministry on transforming society, inviting people to begin living as though the reign (or kingdom) of God were now among them. Faithful to the prophetic tradition, Jesus teaches that God's reign—that is, where God's will is done—overturns society's deepest assumptions about who matters most and who matters least. Jesus is known for his disturbingly countercultural values, not because he rejects society, but because he envisions an inclusive and egalitarian community in place of the exclusionary and oppressive societies so common in human history.

Consider, for example, Jesus' scandalous willingness to eat with the most socially reviled and disreputable of his day, people identified as "sinners" and "tax collectors" (i.e., Roman collaborators).[3] As described in the Gospels, Jesus was notorious for his willingness to be the guest of those considered outside the bounds of respectable society. Even though eating does not carry the deep meaning in many of our modern cultures that it had in the ancient Near East, it is still the case, even today, that eating together establishes community. It means something to invite someone home—or to be invited to someone's home—for dinner. And notwithstanding Jesus' example, societal norms still prevent "respectable" Christians from inviting sex workers, drug dealers, or even people of significantly lower social classes to dine with them.

Jesus' focus on restoring community beginning with the marginalized, a sign of the inclusive reign of God, is evident not only in his table fellowship but also in his miracles. These miracles are often taken as evidence of Jesus' compassion for suffering people, and so they are. However, Jesus' miracles are also, and in no small part, concerned with demonstrating the kind of human community that God desires, and this is an important part of the significance (the "sign" quality) of the miracles.

For example, when the crowd remains with Jesus until mealtime is upon them, Jesus' closest disciples encourage him to disperse the crowd and send the people home for their suppers. Who can blame these disciples for feeling a bit overwhelmed at the idea of hosting a dinner party for well over five thousand? Yet Jesus insists on keeping the people together, creating an experience of God's reign as it is so often described in Jesus' parables: a great communal feast with an abundance of food for all.[4]

The healing miracles also demonstrate Jesus' concern, not merely with the recovery of individual health (important though that is), but with the restoration of people to community. Anyone who has suffered a serious illness knows that disease can disrupt relationships, increasing loneliness and isolation. Even in the best of circumstances, the sick are not able to participate fully in the daily life of the community.

The exclusion of the sick is particularly evident in the case of those suffering from what is called leprosy in the New Testament. People with visible skin diseases had to be cured of their "uncleanness" before they could return to even the most casual interactions with others in society. As if to make sure that we do not miss his point, the Gospels tell us that Jesus heals lepers through touching them, even while other gospel stories indicate that Jesus is able to heal without direct contact and from a distance.[5] In touching these "untouchables," Jesus is shown to be challenging their exclusion from society: he voluntarily takes upon himself the social isolation that includes not only lepers but also anyone who has had physical contact with them.

Jesus' point could scarcely be clearer—one cannot follow Jesus and also observe the laws that exclude lepers.

The egalitarian inclusiveness of Jesus' ministry—especially his shockingly open table fellowship—no doubt informed the early Christian practice of gathering weekly to share a ritual meal together with others in the local Christian community. Though St. Paul himself probably never heard Jesus preach, St. Paul knew enough about the Jesus movement to insist that this Christian meal could not, at the same time, honor Jesus and replicate the social hierarchies that separate people. In his First Letter to the Corinthians, St. Paul reminds Jesus' followers in Corinth that their weekly meal—the forerunner of the eucharistic sharing of bread and wine by Christians today—requires the same rejection of social divisions that Jesus demanded. If this is the Lord's Supper, then all must be equal, with no distinction between the rich and the poor (see 1 Cor 11:17–24).

As St. Paul's letters (the oldest texts in the New Testament) further demonstrate, early Christians understood their sharing of the Lord's Supper to be the celebration of a "new" covenant, a covenant in and through Jesus that forms his followers into a people so tightly bound together that they are one body—the Body of Christ in the world.[6] While all meals join together those who share a common table, this ritual meal is celebrated as a sacrament that unites all present with each other and with God.

The eucharistic sharing of food (now usually just bread and wine instead of the full meal of the early Christian communities) also explicitly commemorates Jesus' final dinner with his friends, the night before he died. All four of the canonical Gospels specify that Jesus' "last supper" took place during the Passover season. This underscores the connection between the Christian meal giving thanks for God's gift of redemption in Jesus Christ and the Jewish Passover meal celebrating God's gift of freedom from slavery in Egypt.

The proclamation that the wine is "the blood of the covenant," along with the Western Christian tradition of using unleavened bread (like the bread eaten at Passover), reinforce this link between the Christian eucharistic covenant and the Exodus event that culminated in the Mosaic covenant. The Christian hope for the redemption of all in Jesus Christ is thus connected to the Jewish laws that seek to contribute to the repair of the world's division and disharmony, in the hope that all will one day flourish in a just community, in harmony with God, and in an abundant land.

CHRISTIAN TRADITION: PERSONS-IN-COMMUNITY

For two millennia, Christianity has upheld the biblical view of human beings as persons-in-community rather than as individuals sufficient unto themselves. This Christian tradition maintains that humans are, by nature, social beings that can develop fully only in relationships with others. The biblical concern with just and healthy communities is thus seen as rooted in our nature as social creatures.

The former pope and recently proclaimed saint, John Paul II, often cited the story of the creation of humanity as evidence that God made human beings to be relational. As St. John Paul II reminded people, in Genesis 2:18, God declared that "it is not good that the man should be alone," and so eventually made a human couple, each oriented to the other. People develop into their true selves only when they are able to give of themselves to others in "a sincere gift of self," as John Paul II frequently taught (see especially *Mulieris Dignitatem*).[7]

For Americans inclined to view community as a threat to individuality, it seems odd—if not thoroughly wrongheaded—to claim that human beings develop fully only by giving of themselves to others. Is this not a sacrifice of the self, the opposite of self-realization?

Yet when I ask students whether they have ever known anyone who is fundamentally happy and fulfilled—not of course someone without any pain or sorrow, but someone who is nevertheless deeply content and at peace—those who know such a person invariably describe someone more concerned about others than about him/herself.

The lives of the saints similarly suggest that self-giving love fulfills rather than destroys the self. St. Francis of Assisi, for example, with his joyful and extravagant love of God, others, and nature, could not be further from our image of an insipid, homogenous holiness in which the person's uniqueness is sacrificed. In spending his life in love, St. Francis—like the other saints whose stories we remember—did not lose his individuality but rather became his compelling and thoroughly distinct self. Devotion to such saints, to those who, like St. Francis, lived an abundantly self-giving love, flourishes still today because people continue to be attracted to these vividly unique and creative personalities. The many saints celebrated throughout the liturgical year present us with a diversity of personalities and a variety of examples of how to live a life of self-giving love. They are surely evidence that Christian discipleship encourages rather than suppresses the development of one's distinctness as a person.

This understanding of human beings as intended for loving relations is the context in which the Christian tradition's emphasis on the two "greatest" commandments is best understood. Of course, Jesus is remembered as having taught that the greatest commandments are to love God with all one's heart and soul and to love one's neighbor as oneself or, perhaps better translated, as another self. People are often surprised, however, to learn that the formulation of these two great commandments did not originate with Jesus. Already in Jesus' day, there was a developed Jewish tradition recognizing that the intent of the law is fulfilled in a love that restores harmony with God and in society. This is evident in the Gospel of Luke, where it is not Jesus but the scholar of the Jewish

11

law who announces that the law code teaches this twofold love of God and neighbor, an interpretation with which Jesus agrees (see Luke 10:25–28).

God's laws are not, then, an arbitrary list of obligations meant simply to test our obedience. As understood in the Jewish and Christian traditions, these laws are guides to the social harmony for which we were created and in which we are fulfilled. We are commanded to love because doing so enables us to become the vibrant, unique persons God created us to be. We are truly ourselves only in loving relationship with God and others.

St. Augustine, the brilliant fifth-century bishop and theologian, further enriched our understanding of these commandments. He taught that the goal of Christian life is to love God above all and to love all else in God and for the sake of God.[8] Augustine helps us to see that love of God and love of neighbor are not two separate commandments, but rather one stance of love toward God and toward the world God created. After all, how could one love God without also deeply respecting—indeed loving—the world that God's love sustains in existence? True love of God, as Augustine thus clarifies, does not make people indifferent to others or to the world, but rather empowers us to love creation, humanity, and ourselves properly.

Given this emphasis on love of all God's creation, the Christian tradition has wisely identified pride as the most deadly of sins, deadly to self as well as to society. Instead of turning outward, in love of God and neighbor, the proud turn inward, relating all things to themselves as the center (or "god") of their world. Rather than self-gift, we have self-aggrandizement; in place of serving others, we seek to be served by them. Pride, as the Christian tradition has long maintained, distorts the self as well as the relationships on which the self depends.

Alas, one of the many forms of pride is the religious pride that focuses on one's relation to God apart from others. In his writings on the Eucharist, the former Joseph Ratzinger, who became pope and then pope emeritus Benedict XVI, warned against such individualistic—and pride-filled—distortions of faith. Like a modern St. Paul, Benedict reminded us that the celebration of the Lord's Supper should join together rather than separate the faithful.[9] In the Body of Christ, we are not only united to Christ as our head, but also united to all others who are with us in Christ.

This union in Christ is traditionally called the "communion of saints," in which all who accept God's offer of love (the living as well as the dead!) participate in a web of mutual sharing, or communion, with one another. The fullness of this communion of all in God is nothing less than the reign of God, and so will be complete only at the end of time. Nevertheless, this communion is partially experienced now in the love and mutual help among all the faithful, including those still alive as well as those who have already completed their temporal lives.

SEEKING OUR GOOD IN THE COMMON GOOD

What would it be like if Christians really lived this belief that we are persons-in-community, that the good of each one of us is inseparable from the common good, from the good of all others?

As mentioned above, evidence suggests that many Americans view the common good as an impediment to their personal well-being, rather than as the source of mutual flourishing. We assume that we are a threat to one another, and so, in what becomes a self-fulfilling prophecy, we are. Increasingly, we live walled off from and armed against one another, voting our pocketbooks in an unending race to attain security for ourselves at the expense of others.

This self-centeredness is a problem not only nationally but internationally. As the world is increasingly brought together in trade, communication, travel, and migration, there is perhaps no more pressing question than the question of whether we will find ways to cooperate for the good of all. Must we continue our desperate competition against each other, hoping that others, and not ourselves, will be the losers, deprived of the world's resources and riches? Or might we find the courage to risk putting the good of others and even of the world as whole before our own short-term personal gain?

In a divided humanity plagued by desperate (and now global) competition, it may well seem unrealistic to strive for the common good rather than personal success. Are we demanding too much if we ask Christians to sacrifice their immediate personal interests to the good of their communities, their nations, and indeed the whole world? Is it not more reasonable—and safer—to seek only moderate social reforms that don't risk too much of one's own interests in this harsh world?

Yet maybe the reverse is true. Perhaps, as Howard Thurman argued, the church is weakened not by asking too much of people but by asking too little of them. Despite his personal experience of the tenacity of racism, Thurman refused to believe that white Southern churches had to compromise with segregation to retain their members. To the contrary, Thurman argued, if churches truly exemplified the love of all, a love that accepts everyone—without exception—as precious brothers and sisters, people would flock to these churches to learn their secret of how to live together in love and peace.[10] After all, people once gathered in crowds to hear Jesus' invitation to live as though the reign of God were a reality, as though it were possible to live as if God and not the powerful Roman Empire governed their lives.

The question remains before us and can only be answered in practice. How deeply might our divided communities, our polarized nation, and our conflict-ridden world be changed if Christians were to live as if they truly believe what they claim: that the good of others is integral—rather than opposed—to each person's own well-being?

Chapter 2

EMBRACING INDIVIDUALITY AND DIVERSITY

OUR FOCUS THUS FAR has been on recovering community amid the hyper-individualism of contemporary American culture. But there is an opposite and equally undesirable error: the collectivism that stifles individuality and values the person only as a contributor to the well-being of a homogenous group.

Recall a lively party you have enjoyed, or a successful meeting you have participated in. The group must have shared quite a bit in common. Too much difference and the party is awkward and strained; a group's work stalls without common understandings to build on. Yet at the same time, some difference is crucial. A party without distinct personalities lacks life, and a meeting whose members all think alike produces dull and undistinguished results.

So, even while there is security in being alike, we know that human beings do not thrive in a monotonous uniformity. Like social events and work groups, a community that includes and encourages diversity without becoming factionalized is more interesting—and healthier—than a community of stifling conformity.

Recognizing the diversity inherent in the world, Christianity has affirmed that God's plan is for a dynamic unity-in-diversity, a harmony that unites people in their differences rather than making them all the same. The human race is enhanced by its variety of peoples and cultures; similarly, each community should be enriched by the individuality of its members.

We fail to understand the Christian emphasis on persons-in-community, then, when a commitment to greater unity is thought to require a uniformity that suppresses difference. This is a serious mistake; uniformity is not unity. Uniformity requires sameness, whereas unity seeks to establish harmony amid diversity. After all, where there is only an undifferentiated sameness, there is nothing to unite.

It might seem that denial of distinctness is not much of a temptation in the United States, given the American emphasis on individuality. Apart from the occasional flare-up of cults and sectarian religious groups offering a cohesive community to those who feel unmoored, Americans are seldom explicitly encouraged to temper their individuality. Yet as the mind-numbing sameness of the ubiquitous "selfie" photos suggests, Americans do face pressures to suppress their differences and be like everyone else.

One common way in which U.S. society undermines the value of individual distinctness is by treating as disposable those who do not conform to the demands of our economy. Consider the many who are pushed to the margins of society: the homeless, the mentally ill, the unemployed, the elderly poor. These "unproductive" people are deprived of a place in society and in its web of supportive relationships. Many become more or less invisible people living in the shadows of our cities, ignored as insignificant, or worse, shunned as subhuman. Such people are perceived by the larger society as a problem to be controlled rather than as people whose absence from the community is regretted and whose company and contributions are missed.

And everyone who witnesses this marginalization learns a grim lesson: those who are not able to contribute to the economy are of little value to this society.

Another common devaluing of individual distinctness is evident in the pressure on women to sacrifice themselves for the good of others, especially in the family. Throughout much of the twentieth century, married women who sought to cultivate themselves and their talents outside of the home were explicitly accused of the sin of pride, one of the most serious of Christian sins. They were told that their role was to support the development of their children and husbands, not to foster their own talents or personal development.

With nearly 70 percent of mothers working outside the home in the United States today, many assume that such attitudes have disappeared.[1] Yet the pressure on women continues, as is evident in the "mommy wars": the ongoing social criticism of women as self-indulgent, regardless of whether they pursue careers, stay at home to raise their children full time, or choose not to have children.

To be sure, sustaining families and raising children requires a considerable willingness to sacrifice one's own comfort and desires. Anyone who has dragged him- or herself out of a deep sleep to feed a screaming baby will attest to this. Relationships require self-sacrifice for the good of others, especially when some of those others cannot care for themselves.

But shouldn't family life be where we practice sharing in the trade-offs necessary to encourage the development of each member as well as the good of the whole? Regardless of whether mothers work in or outside of the home, they should not be expected to give disproportionately while the rest of the family enjoys the benefits. This teaches children to devalue women's potential, and denies them an opportunity to experience mutuality. Instead of practicing the true reciprocity of persons-in-community, they learn that some must do the sacrificing, while others receive the benefits.

Yet another, and one of the most pernicious, denials of the distinct value and worth of persons is expressed in the discrimination minorities face on a daily basis. Despite the robust rhetoric of equality in American society, racial, ethnic, and gender discrimination and violence continue to be all too real, along with subtle—and sometimes not so subtle—pressures to conform to the ways of the dominant group. At one level of extreme violence, we have the criminalization of Black bodies to the point that unarmed Black men are regularly perceived (and killed!) as lethal threats even to armed and trained police. In a more quotidian example, the U.S. Army recently featured African American servicewomen in their advertisements, while imposing hairstyle restrictions that assumed Caucasian hair to be normative.[2] The appearance of diversity is fostered, but true diversity, the diversity that might disrupt established assumptions and power dynamics, is suppressed.

However much Americans enjoy "ethnic" foods and the idea of a multicultural and multiracial society, we still live, go to school, socialize, and worship with those who are most like ourselves. This is not surprising. After all, it's not easy to bridge differences, and there is considerable comfort in sharing a foundation of common experience and expectation. Perhaps the greatest comfort for those in the majority is the assumption that the dominant culture is not only normative but natural and just, an assumption that goes unchallenged when there are sufficient barriers to acknowledging any experience that questions the status quo. Dominant groups can then ignore the reality of social conformity demanded even in a society explicitly committed to celebrating the distinctness of the individual.

Racial, ethnic, gender, and religious discrimination are not, of course, limited to the United States. A cursory glance at the newspaper headlines on nearly any day will reveal that achieving community together amid our differences is a worldwide problem and one of the greatest challenges of our day. Globalization is increasing travel, communication, trade, and migration, all of which bring together ideas and practices as well as people, calling into question established customs and power dynamics. In response, anti-immigration movements are growing in many countries, and outbreaks of violence between different ethnic, racial, and religious groups are common.

Learning to live as persons-in-community, incorporating difference into a vibrant harmony, is both crucially important and increasingly difficult in this global age.

THE BIBLE: FROM BABEL TO PENTECOST

As we discussed in the first chapter, the Hebrew Bible and the New Testament focus on communities: the community of Israel and of the Jesus movement that became the church. Yet these biblical communities are not depicted as requiring total conformity or as valuing persons only insofar as they contribute to the greater good of the whole. Even while the Bible focuses on social harmony and justice, the Bible also includes stories that reinforce the value of the distinct person.

Consider the stories in which God answers Abraham's questioning of divine justice, responds to Rebecca's distress about her difficult pregnancy, fulfills Moses' desire to see at least the backside of God, and responds to Job's plea for an explanation of his suffering, to note just a few instances (see Gen 18:16–33; 25:20–23; Exod 33:18–23; Job 38—41). The person's role in the community or in the divine plan is evidently not all that matters here—God is also concerned with the personal anguish of specific people.

The Mosaic Law provides further evidence that the community is expected to respect the value of the person and his or her claims on society. The poor have a right to be cared for, foreigners deserve to be welcomed, and the hungry must be allowed access to grain left unharvested in the fields (see Exod 22—23). Another intriguing example of the rights of the person is the legal exemption of a bridegroom from the obligation to join other men in battle during a time of war (Deut 24:5). Apparently, the community's security does not outweigh the significance of the groom's personal transition to married life and family responsibilities.

God's concern for each person is also clearly affirmed in Jesus' announcement to his audience that God has numbered the hairs on their heads (Luke 12:7; Matt 10:30). In the Gospel of Luke, Jesus further clarifies that it is not only good people, the ones who do

DIVINE HARMONY

God's will, who are the subjects of divine concern. Rather, we are told, God is like the shepherd who leaves the flock to find one stray sheep, or the housekeeper who sweeps the whole house to find her lost coin. Indeed, among the most moving biblical declarations of God's love is the claim that there is more joy in heaven over one repentant sinner than over all the righteous (see Luke 15:1–10). God, as here described, deeply desires that each person be brought back into relationship with God and included in the harmonious community God is building.

That God yearns for the flourishing of persons in diverse communities is especially apparent when one considers together the biblical accounts of the Tower of Babel and of Pentecost. The story of the Tower of Babel, in Genesis 11, completes the account of the transformation of God's creation from a good and harmonious world into the difficult, often inhospitable, and conflict-ridden reality we live in. As the story begins, the people are all living together and marshaling their combined talents to build a tower that will reach the heavens and demonstrate their power. God responds to this human initiative by "confusing" their languages so that the people cannot understand each other and are unable to work together. They abandon the tower and their attempts to live together, sorting themselves into distinct linguistic groups and spreading throughout the world. Difference has been introduced, and humanity is divided.

On the surface level of the story, the various languages are a divine punishment, presumably for having attempted to rival God. However, a deeper look at the story of Babel Tower, especially in the context of the preceding chapters of Genesis, reveals that something else may be going on here. God has twice commanded the people to fill the earth, yet here they still are in Genesis 11, huddled together like children afraid to leave the security of the group and the familiarity of known territory.[3]

Given this failure to venture out into the larger world, perhaps the diversity of languages is not so much a punishment as it is a further prompt, a divine goad to get the people on their way. Once

the languages are diversified, the people do as they have been commanded and spread throughout the world, forming many nations
with distinct cultures.

In an echo of the story of the Tower of Babel, the account of
Pentecost in the New Testament begins with the nascent Christian
community huddling together after the ascension of Jesus, afraid to
begin the task of going forth into the world. As described in Acts 2,
the apostles are still all together in Jerusalem when they are sud-
denly filled with the Holy Spirit in the form of wind and flames.
Empowered and emboldened by the Spirit of God, they emerge
to share the story of Jesus fearlessly with the world. Remarkably,
we are told, the people present in Jerusalem from different countries each hear the apostles speaking in their own language. Many
convert, and the new church community increases in diversity, a
diversity that continues to grow as the disciples spread the gospel
throughout the world.

Significantly, Pentecost affirms rather than negates the plural-
ity of languages established in Genesis. Diversity is not a punishment that will be rescinded; nor is diversity an aspect of the fallen
human condition that will be overcome with some new cultural-
linguistic uniformity. Instead, the linguistic variety remains, yet is
no longer an obstacle to mutual understanding or to community.
The Holy Spirit unites the community in and through the differences that were apparently part of God's plan all along.

A similar appreciation of difference is evident in St. Paul's
advice to early Christian communities. Even while he defends the
equal dignity of all members of the church, he emphasizes the proper
diversity of Christian roles and contributions. As he explains in his
letter to the community at Corinth, the church is the Body of Christ
and, like a physical body comprised of various parts, the Christian
body must also be differentiated. "For just as the body is one and
has many members, and all the members of the body, though many,
are one body, so it is with Christ. For in the one Spirit we were all

baptized into one body—Jews or Greeks, slaves or free—and we were all made to drink of one Spirit" (1 Cor 12:12–13).

Paul clearly does not envision the church as a community in which all are the same—like a body composed of a single organ. Rather than enforcing a stifling uniformity, the church should welcome and celebrate the various gifts and contributions of the members who make up the complex and differentiated body of the church.

At the same time, the different roles and talents must not become reasons for strife. A body whose parts do not work together is not merely dysfunctional: such a body is sick and at risk of death. Hence, Paul opposes any factionalism that would divide the community, even while he vigorously defends the diversity that enriches the whole.

The church's mission is not to overcome diversity, then, but to embrace it, uniting humanity in a loving harmony that values rather than stifles difference.

CHRISTIAN TRADITION: DIVERSITY IN COMMUNITY

As is suggested by the story of Pentecost and the writings of St. Paul, the Christian movement became diverse early in its history. The new church understood its mission to be universal, and so decided that Gentiles could become full members of the Christian community without becoming Jews (Gal 2). This decision ensured that the church community included differences even on such fundamental matters as what is considered to be acceptable food, since Gentile Christians did not keep kosher as Jewish Christians did.

Recognizing the infinite worth of each person offered everlasting life with God, the church also sought and accepted converts from all classes and states of life as well as ethnicities. Slaves were included along with their masters, even though, unfortunately, their equality in the eyes of the church evidently did not extend beyond church gatherings. A variety of vocations and styles of life were also honored in the early church, as married couples were welcomed along with the celibate, hermits as well as those who sought monastic communities, itinerant preachers and those who remained in their home cities. This acceptance of diversity has been integral to the church's self-understanding through the centuries (at least in theory if not always in practice). Sent to all nations, the church is and must be open to all.

The immense value of each person in his or her distinctness is further underscored by the often-neglected Christian belief in a bodily resurrection. Although Christians throughout the world recite the Nicene Creed and affirm their hope in the "resurrection of the dead," this belief is often overlooked as Christians instead imagine a nonbodily afterlife. However, as St. Paul argued, Jesus rose bodily from the dead not as *sui generis*, one of a kind, but as the "first fruit" whose resurrection promises a bodily fullness of life for all the faithful beyond death. ("If Christ has not been raised, your faith is futile and you are still in your sins. Then those also who have died in Christ have perished. If for this life only we have hoped in Christ, we are of all people most to be pitied. But in fact Christ has been raised from the dead, the first fruits of those who have died" [1 Cor 15:17–20].)

This belief in a bodily resurrection is widely disregarded in part, no doubt, because it is difficult to grasp. There are no clear answers to questions about what kind of physical reality this resurrected body will have, or how it might be related to the body that decomposes or is cremated. Christians have traditionally assumed that our resurrected bodies will be like that of Jesus as described in the New Testament resurrection stories: similar to our current bodies in being able to be touched and to eat, yet different in being able to pass through locked doors. Exactly what kind of physicality this is remains unknown.

Bodily resurrection is also neglected because it just isn't obvious to many today what difference this belief makes. Despite our contemporary obsession with bodies, with maintaining and improving the appearance, the fitness, and the health of our bodies, somehow we still don't understand the ancient Christian (and Jewish) wisdom that our bodies are integral to our distinct identities.

Yet bodies are one of the clearest markers of individuality. We recognize one another and are recognized most easily by physical appearance or by the distinct sounds of our voices. As bodily beings, we have a particular set of characteristics and abilities; we inherit one set of genes rather than another, so we are tall or short, athletic or uncoordinated, with curly or straight hair. In affirming that human beings rise bodily from the dead, the church is teaching not only the hope for an everlasting life with God, but also that people in the afterlife continue to be distinct individuals.

According to the Christian tradition, the afterlife is not then one in which all merge into an undifferentiated unity. Rather, each person retains his or her full and, in some manner, physical uniqueness for eternity.

This personal distinctness, so treasured by God that it is given eternal life, should also be valued in society and especially in the church. Christian faith affirms that each unique person enriches the church community, bringing specific gifts for the building up of the church and its mission to the world. For this reason, the faith community has a responsibility to help each person discern his or her gifts and how they might best be used for the good of the church and for the world.

This discernment of gifts is an important aspect of church life that is easily lost when churches become so large that members feel anonymous, unknown to each other, and unable to contribute. When this happens, the church becomes more like a dispensary of spiritual goods and services to consumers, rather than a community enriched by the mutual sharing of all in the unity of the Holy Spirit.

One group that has maintained an emphasis on the importance of each person's contribution is the Religious Society of Friends, more commonly known as Quakers. Committed to the belief in what they call "that of God in every one," Quakers emphasize that each person not only has irreducible dignity and value but also has personal insight into some part of the ultimate truth that cannot be grasped in any one perspective. Quakers thus practice prayerful dialogue as a discipline of consensus building, listening carefully to each voice in search of the greater truth that reconciles all perspectives. The community moves forward only when all views have been considered and agreement has been achieved in and through the exploration of different views.

It is also because Quakers believe that there is God in everyone that they affirm pacifism. They appeal to the divine in the other as the basis for establishing common ground in cases of conflict, refusing the coercion that would silence opposing perspectives.

Most Christian churches are considerably larger than intimate Quaker gatherings, and so find it difficult to achieve unity without enforcing uniformity or to embrace diversity without falling into division. The Catholic Church, with its emphasis on unity, is often tempted to suppress legitimate diversity in favor of uniformity. The ministry of the pope is important in this regard, because it is his particular responsibility to be the great bridge builder (*pontifex maximus*), the one who ensures that differences within the church remain in unity and contribute to the good of the whole church. At times, unfortunately, the power of a centralized papacy has led the Catholic Church to set rules enforcing a global uniformity that stifles rather than preserves differences.

Protestants have tended to err in the other extreme. Encouraging Christians to interpret the Bible for themselves, the resulting diversity of opinions has often become a source of church division rather than a contribution to mutual enrichment. Individual authenticity is then achieved at the expense of church unity.

Yet both Protestants and Catholics recognize the continuing presence of the Holy Spirit working to unite Christians amid our differences. The ecumenical movement continues to advance not only through official dialogue but, more importantly, through ordinary

Christians finding ways to work and to pray together despite belonging to different denominations.

One important contribution of the ecumenical movement is renewed attention to the ancient Christian (and especially Orthodox) understanding of the church as a communion of churches, or, perhaps better, a communion of communions. That is, the church is not best described as a single entity but rather as a multilayered reality, a community composed of distinct communities that are themselves made up of yet smaller communities (including the family).[4] Each particular church is a full instance of the church, gifted with the Holy Spirit and formed to be the Body of Christ in and for the world. At the same time, each particular church with its own customs is understood as joined to all other churches in this same unifying Spirit, as part of the one indivisible Body of Christ. Layers of difference within and among church communities are thus acknowledged and honored while the ultimate unity of the church is maintained.

It is as this communion of communions that the church carries out its universal mission, seeking to incorporate an ever-broader array of differences into an ever-deeper unity. Valuing the enormous diversity of God's creation and the uniqueness of each infinitely precious person, the church at its best resists understanding itself as a single, monolithic community. Instead, when the church embraces its calling to be a communion of diverse and mutually enriching communities, Christians together witness to a unity that is not uniformity—until the time foretold by Isaiah when all the nations will come together at the mountain of the Lord and there will be peace on earth (see Isa 2:1–4).

EMBRACING THE UNIQUENESS OF SELF AND OTHERS

Years ago, when I was just out of college, I heard a sermon in which the priest declared that everyone we have ever met is a part of us. I don't know why the idea struck me so much that I remember it decades later. I'm usually hard-pressed to recall the topic of last week's homily (which I must confess I've sometimes forgotten by the end of the service). Perhaps it was the novelty of the claim; this was a new idea to me, and at the time I could not say whether I thought it was true or not.

In the years since, I have come to appreciate the wisdom of this simple truth about the depth of our influence on one another. In the turns of phrase I have picked up from one person, in a gesture or insight I learned from another, I find in my daily life and my very being traces of the influence of people I have not seen for years. And, of course, there is the deeper reality of being formed by culture, language, traditions of knowledge, and practices that have developed through millennia. We are indeed a part of one another—made to be bound together in relationships in which each person contributes uniquely to the others and to the common life.

When we take seriously the value of each person and of our mutual interrelatedness, we cannot help but resist both the collectivism that suppresses individuality and the individualism that tears apart community. From the perspective of persons-in-community, life is not a zero-sum game pitting the individual and the community against each other. Rather, it is a process of reciprocal enrichment in which the development of the person contributes to the community, while a truly healthy community fosters the personal growth of its members.

Many have (rightly) recognized that this Christian emphasis on the value of each person encourages support for human rights. Some Christians, however, have recently rejected attention to human rights as an unchristian individualism; they believe that human rights language fails to appreciate the priority of community and of social relationships. But this is a mistake: the rejection of human rights falls into just that dichotomous thinking that a persons-in-community approach resists. Rather than choosing between the rights of the person and the requirements of the community, the Christian tradition would have us recognize that persons develop best in a society that respects and protects the proper freedom of its members, who in turn strengthen their society. An increase in individual rights need not undermine society; nor should greater social bonds decrease individuality.

Of course, a Christian understanding of human rights also contrasts with the libertarian view in which society protects the rights of individuals only to the point of establishing a level playing field of competition, with an attitude of "devil take the hindmost." To be sure, fairness in competition is an important value, and some aspects of society may be best organized competitively. But society as a whole is not a competition and—if what Christianity holds is true—society does not flourish when it pits its members against one another. Christian endorsement of the rights and freedoms that allow personal development should not come at the expense of social structures of mutual support.

In contrast to an emphasis on competition that undermines both person and community, Christianity calls us to attend to the dignity of each person sustained in relationships of mutuality. Practicing such attention will lead to greater awareness of the extent to which all of us are diminished when some are excluded from the community. The many people treated as disposable, the homeless, mentally ill, and all others who are thrust to the margins of society, need adequate food, shelter, and medical care, of course, but they—and we—also need their inclusion in society. The marginalized are diminished by not having opportunities to give to and to receive from the community, while the rest of society is diminished by the loss of the unique presence and contributions of these excluded people.

Appreciation of the value of persons should also encourage Christians to resist denigration of the self, which is as much of a contradiction of true self-gift as is an overly proud or narcissistic disposition. While Christianity has traditionally focused on the sin of pride, some have persuasively argued in recent decades that women are often more inclined to the sin of self-loss. Certainly, both extremes fail to achieve the genuine giving of self, because the self must be cultivated in order to be a true gift. Developing the self is not selfishness or arrogance, then, but rather is the basis for mutual enrichment. Neglecting the self, on the other hand, diminishes both the person and the community that suffers the loss of that person's potential.

Perhaps especially in our overworked, 24/7 society, Christians would do well to attend to the importance of proper self-development. The Gospels tell us that Jesus withdrew periodically to pray, and he praised Mary of Bethany for caring for her own spiritual development even when her sister could have used her help (see Luke 10:38–42). Surely not only women, but all of us today must learn to resist the endless petty demands and the distractions that threaten to block our personal growth.

Of course, truly valuing the dignity of every person, self and others, requires accepting all the personal, linguistic, and cultural diversity that each brings to the community. But this is not easy. As the evidence of seemingly insurmountable tensions between people of different religions, ethnicities, races, and cultures suggests, real diversity can be uncomfortable. Unfamiliar cultural practices and assumptions are confusing and may lead to deep misunderstanding. We fear that we will find ourselves pushed out and our places taken by those we welcomed in. Or perhaps more diversity will undermine the common ground that holds the community itself together.

To some extent, these are risks we must take, inspired by the recognition that we are not OK without one another. If we know, deep down, that we are diminished by the divisions among us—if we truly believe that the Holy Spirit is at work to unite us in our differences—then we may yet find the courage to risk opening ourselves and our beloved communities to the greater diversity that is God's will and that could enrich us beyond our imagining.

Chapter 3

REDEEMED—TOGETHER

"JESUS SAVES!" The preacher was at his usual corner on Chicago's State Street, shouting through his bullhorn to attract the attention of passing crowds. Rushing to catch my train home, I gave little more than a quick glance at this dedicated man. He was there most days, blasting his message to indifferent pedestrians more focused on escaping the rain, snow, or just the sharp, wet wind so common in the late afternoon in Chicago. Few were interested in his offer of salvation.

A few blocks farther south, in front of the Pacific Garden Mission, "Jesus Saves" was lit in neon lights in the shape of a cross. This too was hardly remarkable. Like the corner preacher with the bullhorn, announcements of salvation appear frequently on billboards and marquees in American cities. Most of us prefer to keep this message at a distance, avoiding the evangelizers who approach and ask, in a tone that combines threat and promise, "Are you saved?"

As common as the proclamation of salvation through Jesus is, seldom does anyone bother to explain what this salvation is all about. What are we saved from, or what are we saved for? I suppose both preachers and passersby think the answer is obvious: salvation is about avoiding everlasting torture in hell, and achieving instead eternal bliss in heaven. Christian salvation, we often assume, is a matter of one's personal destiny: the "saved" get an afterlife of unending happiness rather than the utter misery everyone else will have.

Yet if we are inherently a part of one another—if we are truly persons-in-community and not solitary individuals—then there is something not quite right about this individualistic approach to Christian redemption. If we cannot become who we are meant to be apart from others, then being saved or redeemed by oneself makes little sense. How can we be saved as individuals when we are social beings, made for community?

Walter Rauschenbusch, the great nineteenth- and early-twentieth-century Baptist theologian (whom we'll discuss further in chapter 4), taught a different, more communal, view of salvation. He told a wonderful story about the final judgment, in which it is centuries rather than individuals that are judged. In this modern parable, invented a few years into the twentieth century, the nineteenth century appears among the other centuries and brags about its accomplishments, swaggering a bit as it describes the increase in knowledge and the inventions that enable people to produce more and cheaper goods. However, this newly completed century is soon humbled: it learns that God is less concerned with increasing the advantages of the privileged than with ending the oppression of the poor. The nineteenth century recognizes that it failed in this regard, and admits sorrowfully to the other centuries, "My great cities are as yours were. My millions live from hand to mouth. Those who toil longest have least. My thousands sink exhausted before their days are half spent. My human wreckage multiplies."[1] At this point, the nineteenth century takes its place sadly among the previous centuries, repenting its lost opportunities and misspent energies.

Rauschenbusch created this parable to help Christians envision a less individualistic approach to salvation, one that is more adequate to the Bible and the Christian tradition. After all, Christians focused on their personal afterlife have little basis for appreciating the biblical emphasis on God's interest in justice within history. Why should there be a chosen people at all, and why would

God be involved in—and make judgments on—the political history of that people, if the only point is to get individuals into heaven?

But yet, the biblical prophets are deeply concerned with unjust rulers. Consider Jeremiah, for example, who sends King Zedekiah the message, "Hear the word of the LORD, O King of Judah sitting on the throne of David—you, and your servants, and your people who enter these gates. Thus says the LORD: Act with justice and righteousness, and deliver from the hand of the oppressor anyone who has been robbed. And do no wrong or violence to the alien, the orphan, and the widow, or shed innocent blood in this place" (Jer 22:2–3).

Without a communal sense of salvation, this prophetic emphasis on social justice seems odd, if not misplaced. Similarly, when our focus is on the drama of the individual struggling between good and evil, it's hard to understand why the church matters so much that the early Christians would sell all their property and give the proceeds to the Christian community, as described in the Book of Acts (see especially 4:32–35). Most of the Bible just doesn't fit with our contemporary preoccupation with getting individual souls into heaven.

An individualistic redemption is also troubling because it suggests that our public lives and history are religiously unimportant. If salvation concerns only one's personal afterlife in heaven or hell, what is the point of all that we do to enrich life in this world? Is there any ultimate value to all of the efforts spent increasing beauty and knowledge, or in building just structures and more equitable social systems? Are all of the great historical achievements in art, culture, and politics simply a way to pass time on earth, a sort of "basket weaving" to occupy us as we await our eternal destiny?[2]

This devaluing of history is particularly problematic today, given the magnitude of the challenges the human race is facing. Global capitalism is destabilizing local economies and increasing inequality, triggering worldwide population migrations and making many vulnerable to the new global slave trade. The demand for energy to fuel this consumerist economy has initiated a total global climate change, threatening the conditions of life on this planet. As

Pope Francis has observed, "Whatever is fragile, like the environment, is defenseless before the interests of a deified market, which become the only rule" (*Evangelii Gaudium* 56).[3]

It will take a great deal of effort and worldwide cooperation to tackle these global crises successfully. Yet without confidence that what happens in history is truly significant, there is little motivation to commit the necessary effort to these (and so many other) important issues. Why bother to spend precious time and energy on matters of little consequence?

On the other hand, if God is acting through history to bring all to salvation—and inviting us to cooperate with this divine plan—then surely the sociopolitical challenges of our time must be of considerable religious importance.

Returning to the Bible and to the broader Christian tradition, we do indeed find more support for a social and historical understanding of salvation than for the individualistic approach of much contemporary Christianity. Emphasizing God's redeeming presence in history and in the relationships that bind us to one another, the Bible and other classic Christian sources envision a communal redemption, assuring us that humanity does not struggle alone—or in vain—in its endeavor to transform history and society.

THE BIBLE: HOPE FOR HARMONY

Many people are surprised to learn that the Hebrew Bible (the Christian Old Testament) has scarcely any concept of a personal afterlife. These ancient writings are not concerned with an individual's life after death, but rather with the flourishing of the people of Israel in their land. The future of the community takes precedence over the future of the individual. Moreover, when a personal hope is considered in the Hebrew Bible, the attention is not on surviving death but rather on achieving the good fortune of a long life and many descendants (see Ezek 37:1–14).[4]

Late in the Hebrew Bible, at the end of the Book of Daniel (12:1–3), there is a brief mention of personal afterlife, but even this is not the disembodied spiritual existence that Christians often imagine. Rather, the life after death described here is one in which the just are resurrected to life on this earth, presumably joining with those still alive at the end of history as they celebrate their deliverance from the oppressive and idolatrous rule of the Seleucid dynasty.

The hope of the Hebrew Bible is thus a thoroughly social hope, a hope for the future of the people of Israel along with, occasionally, a further hope that the whole world will be brought into perfect harmony one day. An especially eloquent description of this universal hope for harmony is found in the Book of Isaiah (and echoed in the Book of Micah), in what has been called the vision of the peaceable kingdom.[5]

Of course, the Book of Isaiah, like other books of prophecy in the Hebrew Bible, is mostly concerned with the political and social situation at the time of its authors.[6] The majority of the prophecies in this book are not about a far distant future but rather about trusting in God to bring the community to a life of justice and fidelity to God in their land.

In chapter 2, however, Isaiah foresees a future of perfect justice and harmony among all nations. The major features of this peaceable kingdom include universal worship of God and unending peace among humanity. United in obedience to the God of Israel, humanity will have achieved a peace so firmly established that there will be no need for weapons ("they shall beat their swords into plowshares") or even to learn military strategy ("neither shall they learn war any more") (Isa 2:4).

In chapter 11, Isaiah further develops his description of this peaceable kingdom, envisioning a transformation of nature as well as of society. The world will be so harmonious that children will be able to play near poisonous snakes without giving their parents cause for alarm. Predators will be at peace with their prey, having become vegetarians so that "the wolf shall live with the lamb." Indeed, "they will not hurt or destroy on all my holy mountain" (Isa 11:6, 9).

DIVINE HARMONY

God's ultimate plan, as predicted by Isaiah, does not involve an escape from this world or from our history, but rather a perfection of the world at the end of the history of human struggles. This transformation will return creation to a state quite similar to the Garden of Eden. Recall the early chapters of the Book of Genesis, which describe the first human couple beginning in harmony with each other, with God (who can be found "walking in the garden at the time of the evening breeze" [Gen 3:8]), and with an abundant natural world. In the future Isaiah envisions, the harmony of Eden is restored, as all worship God and live in a peace that excludes even the violence of carnivorous animals.

Isaiah's hope for the perfection of life on earth is echoed in Jesus' preaching of the reign of God in the New Testament. This is especially evident in the Synoptic Gospels; that is, the Gospels of Matthew, Mark, and Luke, which are remarkably similar to each other in the order of events and the stories included.[7] Indeed, the first thing Jesus says in the Gospel of Mark is that he has come to proclaim that God's reign—where all live as God intends—is near (Mark 1:15).

The Gospel of Luke also has Jesus begin his public ministry with an announcement of the good news of God's reign, though Luke includes a more detailed description of this good news. In chapter 4 of Luke's Gospel, Jesus enters the synagogue and reads a short passage from the Book of Isaiah:

> The Spirit of the Lord is upon me,
>   because he has anointed me
>   to bring good news to the poor.
> He has sent me to proclaim release to the captives
>   and recovery of sight to the blind,
>   to let the oppressed go free,
> to proclaim the year of the Lord's favor.
>
> (Luke 4:18–19)

Jesus informs the congregation, "Today this scripture has been fulfilled in your hearing" (Luke 4:21), thus identifying his own mission with the fulfillment of the ancient prophetic hope for freedom, health, and release from the devastation of poverty.

God's reign as portrayed here makes a real difference in people's lives, bringing an end to the suffering of prisoners, the blind, and the poor. Yet this is not an individualistic hope. Freeing captives and bringing good news to the poor indicate a change in society, a point underscored by the proclamation of the year of the Lord's favor. This year of divine favor apparently refers to the jubilee year described in the Book of Leviticus, chapter 25: every forty-nine years, some of the significant gains in inequality over the years are to be reversed through the cancellation of debts and the restoration of family land. When God truly and fully reigns, the people will be united in harmony rather than in systems of subjugation. Indeed, as recounted in the Gospels, one of Jesus' common descriptions of the reign of God is as a grand and joyous banquet with plenty of food and wine (see, e.g., Matt 22:1–14; Luke 14:15–24).

Throughout the centuries and still today, this hope for God's reign is remembered when Christians pray as taught by Jesus in the Gospel of Matthew (6:9–13). In what is often called the "Lord's Prayer" or the "Our Father," we ask that God's kingdom come, that God's will be done *on earth* as it is in heaven.

To be sure, there is a hope for personal resurrection in the New Testament. This idea, introduced into the Hebrew Bible with the Book of Daniel's vision of the rising of the dead, had obviously spread. By the time of Jesus, about 200 years after the Book of Daniel was written, many Jews expected a divine intervention that would not only end history and set all things right, but would also resurrect the dead to share in the joy—or perhaps to experience everlasting shame for betraying their people.

As depicted in the Gospels, Jesus shared this belief in a resurrection of the dead. In one notable story found in all three Synoptic Gospels, the more theologically conservative Sadducees (who apparently did not accept the relatively new belief in resurrection) are intent on pointing out how ridiculous a bodily afterlife is (see Matt 22:23–33; Mark 12:18–27; Luke 20:27–40). They question Jesus about the complications serial marriages would cause for one's marital state in the afterlife. Whose wife would a woman be who had married seven brothers, each on the death of the previous one? Jesus, however, defends bodily resurrection by refusing the assumptions of the question. Our hope for the afterlife, he argues, should not be limited by what we experience in this life: "For in the resurrection they neither marry nor are given in marriage," Jesus answers (Matt 22:30).

A belief in personal resurrection is also evident in Martha's answer at the tomb of her brother Lazarus, as described in chapter 11 of the Gospel of John. When Jesus proclaims that her brother will rise again, Martha responds, "I know that he will rise again in the resurrection on the last day" (John 11:24). As is common at this time, Martha believes there will be a bodily resurrection at the end of history.

It is, of course, the experience of Jesus raised from the dead that establishes resurrection as a central Christian belief. As Paul wrote to the Church of Corinth, "Now if Christ is proclaimed as raised from the dead, how can some of you say there is no resurrection of the dead?" (1 Cor 15:12).

But Jesus' resurrection did not usher in the expected end of history. Indeed, two thousand years after Jesus' resurrection, God's reign is still not here in full. One need only look around to see that God's will is not always done and that life on earth is (obviously!) far from harmonious.

Given this delay in the coming of God's reign, it is understandable that Christians have come to focus on a personal afterlife rather than on a hope for the redemption of history. If Jesus' life, death, and resurrection did not free Israel from Roman occupation and establish justice on earth, perhaps Jesus came to "open the gates of heaven" so that we can enter into an eternal life with God—and escape the problems of this world—when we die.

Yet the New Testament challenges this reduction of the biblical hope for all of history to the anticipation of an individualistic afterlife. Consider that the Book of Revelation, probably written over fifty years after Jesus' death and reported resurrection, ends the Christian Bible with a vision that combines a thoroughly social redemption with the eternal life of the resurrected dead. As described in Revelation 21—22, after all of the dead are raised and judged, the New Jerusalem— a city—descends from the skies to provide a perfect place for the faithful to live together in harmony. All sorrow, suffering, and even death are banished from this city, which shines with precious metals and stones and offers abundant life, with a river of life running through the city and trees of life producing twelve kinds of fruit. Most importantly, there is no need for the sun and stars or any other lights, because God's presence sets the city ablaze with the light of God's glory.

Like the peaceable kingdom of Isaiah, the New Jerusalem envisioned in the Book of Revelation echoes the original creation in the Garden of Eden, with its fertile nature and the absence of suffering and death. Yet again, the awaited end is described as greater even than the idyllic beginning. In place of the Garden of Eden's single tree of life, we find two trees of life bearing ample fruit on either side of the river of life. Instead of a single human couple, we have a great city of people living together in peace. And, of course, while in Genesis God comes intermittently to visit the human couple (and in Isaiah's vision the people worship God on the mountain), now God is continually present in an unmediated glory so profound that there is no longer any need for a specific place of worship.

The creation story in the beginning of Genesis (the first book of the Bible) and the re-creation of the "new heaven and new earth" at the end of Revelation (the last book of the Christian Bible) can be read as framing the Christian imagination of God's plan for humanity. As depicted in the Bible, human beings were created for a life of harmony with each other, with nature, and with God, a harmony that was tragically interrupted by human disobedience. Nevertheless, the Bible promises that at the end of history, after all of the sin, injustice, suffering, and struggle, harmony will be restored and perfected. The dead will be raised so that past generations can join in this glorious reign, the culmination of the long history of the Jewish people, of the ministry of Jesus, of the work of the church, and, indeed, of all of the struggles of humanity.

CHRISTIAN TRADITION: THE UNION OF ALL IN GOD

As Christianity spread throughout the ancient world, further questions arose about who Jesus must be if he is indeed the Savior of humanity, the one who restores the lost harmony with God and with each other. Bishops gathered together in councils and clarified that, if Jesus truly brings a redemptive union with God to humanity, then Jesus must himself be completely united with God.[8] Only by being somehow both fully divine and fully human could Jesus offer to humanity the union with God that overcomes the divisions of sin, setting us right with each other, with nature, and with our true selves as well as with the divine. So, as stated in the Nicene Creed, the bishops of the fourth and fifth centuries clarified the Christian belief that the Lord Jesus Christ is "consubstantial [of one being] with the Father."

Gregory Nazianzus, a fifth-century bishop, confidently expressed this understanding of salvation as the union of God and humanity. "The unassumed is the unhealed, but what is united with God is also being saved," he wrote.[9] In other words, God redeemed humanity in Jesus by taking on (or "assuming") a fully human nature, uniting humanity to God's self. As the twentieth-century Catholic theologian Karl Rahner later explained in terms related to an evolutionary view of history, in Jesus the goal of history (the union of God and humanity) has become established in time so that from Jesus the goal of history spreads through time.[10]

It is not just the death of Jesus that is salvific, then, but rather the entire event of Jesus Christ: his life, death, and resurrection. As described by the second-century bishop Irenaeus of Lyons, Jesus lived a whole human life in unity with God and in full submission to God's will, even through the agony of death and into his new, resurrected life in the fullness of God's reign.[11]

Nevertheless, the death of Jesus has rightly come to hold a central place in Christian devotion. This death was, after all, the culmination of Jesus' life lived in love for humanity and in fidelity to God's will. Jesus did not simply die; he was executed for his faithfulness to his mission. Jesus *could* have avoided Jerusalem and the authorities there who were threatened by his message, or he *might* have preached a less unsettling account of God's will for humanity, accommodating his preaching to what the political reality would tolerate. But he did not choose these easier paths, even though he must have known the danger of so clearly announcing God's reign in the context of Roman imperial rule. Jesus' death was thus the fulfillment of his life spent in union with God's will and love for humanity, rather than in preoccupation with his own safety and well-being.

The death of Jesus further shows that overcoming the disharmony and distortion of sin is no small thing. On the cross, in Jesus' excruciating and humiliating death, God shares in the pain and injustice of human life in a sinful world. Reconciliation, we learn, is not achieved from a safe distance, nor by simply ignoring the past. Broken relationships can only be healed through the difficult work of reestablishing that relationship. So God heals our estrangement by becoming vulnerable and suffering with us, transforming the world from within.

Most importantly, Christians proclaim that Jesus rose from the dead into a new life with God that Jesus offers to the rest of humanity. As celebrated in the sacrament of baptism, Christians are united to Jesus through the power of the Holy Spirit, and thus share already in the power of this resurrected life while growing toward the fullness of union with God. Joined to Jesus, Christians are also, of course, joined to God and to all others in union with God. As St. Paul so well understood, the church is formed to be the Body of Christ, united to one another as the collective presence of Jesus, and bringing his transforming love to the world. Like the people of Israel who were called by God to cooperate with the divine plan to mend the world, the church too has a role in the ongoing history of the world's redemption.

The communal dimension of salvation becomes yet more evident when we consider the Christian doctrine of the Trinity. The ultimate goal of life is not simply to be with or near God, but actually to be taken into the divine life itself. In Jesus, the Word of God (or the Son) became a distinct human being, so there is now the humanity of Jesus, with his particular history, included within the life of the Trinity. If, then, we are united to Jesus, then we too—with all of our distinct histories—are destined to be with Jesus and thus also to be enfolded within the divine, trinitarian love. As triune, God opens God's self to include the diversity of creation within God's own triune life of loving community (see *Laudato Si'* 99, 238–40).[12]

The doctrine of the Trinity is not, then, simply an abstract theological puzzle added to Christian faith. It is a thoroughly salvific doctrine, rooted in the Christian experience of God as revealed in distinct ways in Yahweh, in Jesus, and in the Spirit that enlivens the church and, indeed, the entire world. Yet Christians also affirm the ancient Jewish belief that God is one. To give words to this experience of the ultimate unity of God in loving distinction, the Christian community over the course of a few centuries settled on the concept of God as triune, one God who remains one in three distinct yet inseparable "persons."

Of course, no human metaphor can do justice to the mystery of the divine, but the doctrine of the Trinity is helpful in that it points to the profound Christian belief that God is better described as a loving community than as a solitary individual. Further, since

God is the source of all being, it follows that all that exists shares in God's being and thus is inherently relational, as the Triune God is. Only through growing in loving relationships with others can we become our true selves, then, because we are constituted in our being, as persons, in and through our relationships.

Christian salvation is thus thoroughly relational—we are saved from lonely and loveless lives through God's reconciling presence inviting us to live in the love of God and of all of God's creation. Salvation history is the history of God's offer (and our imperfect human acceptance) of this transforming love, most notably—but not only—in God's covenant with the people of Israel, in Jesus of Nazareth, and in the Spirit Jesus sends to guide his followers.

If we are, in fact, relational beings who become ourselves together with others in and through our histories, then it follows that we can only be redeemed in history. There is no history other than salvation history, as Fr. Gustavo Gutiérrez has astutely noted.[13] That is, there is no place or event in the world in which the grace to love more fully is not offered—though, of course, there are many times and places where that grace is rejected. The history through which we develop as persons-in-community, creating political institutions and struggling to resolve social problems, is also the history through which we are continually invited to overcome our estrangement from God, from each other, from the rest of creation, and finally, from what we are meant to be.

For this reason, the Catholic bishops at the Second Vatican Council made it clear that what we do and suffer in history is part of who we are and so must also somehow be part of the ultimate redemption. As they wrote, "For after we have obeyed the Lord, and in His Spirit nurtured on earth the values of human dignity, brotherhood and freedom, and indeed all the good fruits of our nature and enterprise, we will find them again, but freed of stain, burnished and transfigured, when Christ hands over to the Father: 'a kingdom eternal and universal, a kingdom of truth and life, of holiness and grace, of justice, love and peace'" (*Gaudium et Spes* 39).[14]

43

DIVINE HARMONY

REDEEMING HISTORY

Consider again Rauschenbusch's parable of the judgment of the centuries. What if we imagine the twentieth century—so recently ended—joining the nineteenth and all the previous centuries before the bar of divine judgment? Many of us benefit greatly from the advances of these last hundred years: standards of living have risen, there is more access to education, rights for women and minorities have increased dramatically in many places, and technology enables us to take for granted things that few dreamed of in the past.

Yet the twentieth century was also an extremely violent one, marked by global wars, the development of weapons of mass destruction, and repeated genocides—from the Armenian genocide at the beginning of the century through the mid-century Holocaust of European Jews, to the Rwandan genocide in the century's final years.

The twentieth century also has left us with serious problems of ecological destruction, the impending threat of global climate change, a return of extreme economic inequality in many places, and a growing modern slave trade. In the terms of Rauschenbusch's parable, we can only imagine that the twentieth century was no less humbled by judgment than previous centuries, and that it too joined its sibling centuries in mourning and repentance for its (for our!) failures.

Rauschenbusch's story is a somber goad. Each century has been given the task of bringing God's reign closer, yet each century has failed in significant ways. Dare we hope for better from the twenty-first century? Rauschenbusch reminds us that what truly matters is not technological progress with new gadgets for the amusement of the elite, but overcoming oppression, injustice, and unnecessary human suffering.

This emphasis on judging history from the underside, focusing on the conditions of the poor and the oppressed, interrupts the complacency of the privileged who benefit most from social institutions and from the developments we welcome as progress. It also reminds us of an important truth: human beings cannot and will not achieve the reign of God through our finite, mortal projects. After all, no historic accomplishment of justice, however hard won, is either perfect or permanent. Every system is flawed and every gain may be reversed.

But Christians should not and must not abandon efforts to achieve what they can. Nothing is perfect, but it is crucial that we do not let the inevitability of imperfection become a reason to neglect the good that we can do. After all, whatever we do, or fail to do, makes a difference in our lives and in the lives of those we affect. As Jesus tells his followers in chapter 25 of the Gospel of Matthew, whatever we do or do not do for someone in need, no matter how insignificant that person may seem to be, is done or not done for Jesus himself.

How then can we be indifferent to the people treated as disposable around the world—children living on garbage dumps in the Philippines, for example, or girls sold into sex slavery at home and abroad, or the young African American men facing life imprisonment for nonviolent offenses? It is not only Jesus who shares in the lot of the poor, oppressed, and suffering, after all. As relational beings, intended for an everlasting community together in God, we are all part of one another. If we truly realize this, we will resist the "globalization of indifference" that Pope Francis warns is undermining justice and compassion around the world (*Evangelii Gaudium* 54).

We can also hope that our efforts to create more just and caring societies will contribute somehow to the growth of God's reign. As has been noted by many, the arc of history is long, but it bends toward justice. God's Spirit, which moved over the chaos at creation, is still moving over and through the chaos of our world, empowering people to risk seeking reconciliation in place of division, justice instead of oppression, and mutuality rather than privilege.

Chapter 4

CHRISTIAN SPIRITUALITY

A LOVE THAT DOES JUSTICE

LANGDON GILKEY, who later became an influential Christian theologian, was a young humanist teaching English in China at the outbreak of World War II. Along with other non-Chinese, he was sent to an abandoned missionary camp where the Japanese held foreign nationals during the war. Gilkey reflected deeply on his experiences in the camp and on the lessons he learned there, one of which was that rational arguments seldom persuade people to act against their self-interest for the good of the community. Reasoning about fairness, he learned, was no match for the selfishness of people facing scarcity of food and shelter, even when that selfishness threatened to destroy the community on which they all depended. Their camp did not self-destruct, but only because some members didn't need to be convinced to put the good of the whole group ahead of their personal and immediate well-being. This realization awakened Gilkey's lifelong interest in the formative role of religion in society.[1]

On his return home to the United States, Gilkey was asked to speak to church groups about his years of internment in China. One of the stories he often told was about a time when the American Red Cross learned of their plight and sent more than enough food parcels for the entire camp. Most of the Americans in the camp resisted the demand that the packages be shared equally to supplement the meager rations of all. They maintained that the food belonged to the small group of Americans because the parcels came from a U.S. organization. They even argued that to share the packages equally would be a violation of the sanctity of property rights! This caused so much ill will that the Japanese officials finally intervened, distributed the parcels evenly, and sent the extra ones to another camp.

This was only one of the experiences that caused Gilkey to appreciate the force of self-interest, particularly among people living with little resources. However, Gilkey's church audiences in the United States usually underestimated self-interest's power: they were invariably shocked to learn that Americans had behaved so selfishly, refusing to share with their fellow internees.

Gilkey also noted the overwhelming abundance, especially of food, in the United States during this post-war period. He regularly ended his presentations by asking the audience to support programs assisting the many destitute nations that were still suffering due to the war.

At the conclusion of one of these talks, the leader of the church group that had invited Gilkey smiled with an air of cool superiority and announced that Gilkey misunderstood the purpose of her organization. Even as the table in the adjoining room was being loaded with pastries, cakes, and tea sandwiches to provide refreshments for those gathered, this churchwoman explained that her group was devoted to the "higher" task of fostering spiritual, not physical, well-being. In fact, this group was against economic aid to war-ravaged countries because such aid focused on material development, rather than on the spiritual values that they believed truly matter.

Not surprisingly, Gilkey was unimpressed with the spirituality of these Christians who enjoyed abundance while dismissing others' urgent need for food. It must have sounded to him less like genuine love of neighbor and more like the camp internees' claim that they had to take all of the food packages in order to defend the right to property.

I suspect that few Christians today would divorce the spiritual and the physical as starkly as did the affluent members of this church group. Charity, with its attention to the material needs of others, has been a central Christian practice since the church's earliest days. Moreover, the spiritual value of physical life is affirmed in Christian sacramental practices as well as by the belief in the resurrection of the body.

Still—and with over fifty years of further attention to the importance of social justice in Christian life—there remains a great deal of confusion about what Christian spirituality can or should contribute to a more just social order and a more equitable distribution of the world's resources. As persons-in-community, of course, we cannot ignore the social systems and institutions that organize our common life. These structures are important—they provide the conditions for the relationships that form who we are and become, and too often, these structures benefit some of us at the expense of others. Yet debates about social justice can seem far removed from the generous, loving harmony that Christian faith affirms is our ultimate goal.

Justice, after all, strives to provide what each person is due. Justice thus tends to be impersonal, and usually involves conflict between competing claims. Love, on the other hand, gives generously without regard for what is owed. Love recognizes the unique worth of each person and seeks a harmony in which all flourish together. Compared to love, justice can seem a matter of cool, calculating reason, and as Gilkey found in his camp, reason is seldom sufficient to sustain community.

But how, then, can we best live as responsible persons-in-community now, while looking forward to a more complete communion with God and others than can be achieved in this world? Is it possible for Christians to engage in the often-divisive politics of seeking justice, without sacrificing the love that gives true fulfillment?

More simply put, how should we understand the relation between political justice and Christian love?

THE BIBLE: GOD DESIRES JUSTICE

The Bible, of course, does not support the claim that spiritual values are separate from social justice or from concern for the material needs of the poor. This point is underscored by a creative experiment that noted evangelical author and activist Jim Wallis describes. According to Wallis, a fellow student in his seminary days went through an old Bible, cut out every reference to the poor, and was left with a Bible in shreds. There was barely enough of the book remaining to hold it together. And yet, Wallis notes, American Christianity is too often like this tattered Bible, with responsibility to the poor edited out of the life of faith.[2]

As we saw in chapter 1, the Hebrew Bible, or Christian Old Testament, pays a great deal of attention to the treatment of the poor and, more generally, to the just organization of the community. The laws of the Torah (the first five books of the Bible) govern what is owed not only to God but also to others in society. One example mentioned above is that landowners are not permitted to harvest the entire crop but must leave grain in the fields for the hungry (e.g., Lev 19:9–10; 23:22; Deut 24:19–21). Another law requires that cloaks taken as loan collateral be returned before sundown, so that the poor will not be left without anything to sleep in (see Exod 22:26–27). Indeed, there are repeated admonitions throughout the Torah to care for the widow, the orphan, and the foreigner— those most at risk in a patriarchal, agrarian society. The people are warned that God will smite them—God's own people—if they fail to protect these vulnerable ones as God has protected them (e.g., Exod 22:23–24).

A commitment to equality in a just society is particularly evident in the laws governing the jubilee year. The Book of Leviticus contains the radical stipulation that a jubilee be held every seven times seven (or forty-nine) years, and in this year, all land must be returned to the family that originally owned it. The jubilee year, when observed, would thus reverse much of the inequality of the preceding half century, allowing those who had suffered bad luck to regain their land and have a chance again at independence (see Lev 25:8–10, 28).

God's desire for justice for the poor is, of course, also notable in the prophetic books. Social injustice, along with idolatry, is one of the major covenantal violations the prophets condemn. The prophets Amos and Isaiah even insist that social justice and care for the poor come before the requirements for religious rituals and worship of God. In a passage from the Book of Amos (one that the Rev. Martin Luther King Jr. famously cited during the Civil Rights Movement), God declares,

> Even though you offer me your burnt offerings and
>   grain offerings,
>   I will not accept them;
> and the offerings of well-being of your fatted animals
>   I will not look upon.
> Take away from me the noise of your songs;
>   I will not listen to the melody of your harps.
> But let justice roll down like waters,
>   and righteousness like an everflowing stream.
>
> (Amos 5:22–24)

Isaiah similarly pronounces God's judgment on the people:

> When you stretch out your hands,
>   I will hide my eyes from you;
> even though you make many prayers,
>   I will not listen;
>   your hands are full of blood.

DIVINE HARMONY

Wash yourselves; make yourselves clean;
  remove the evil of your doings
  from before my eyes;
cease to do evil,
  learn to do good;
seek justice,
  rescue the oppressed,
defend the orphan,
  plead for the widow

(Isa 1:15–17)

As Micah nicely summarizes: "And what does the LORD require of you / but to do justice, and to love kindness, / and to walk humbly with your God?" (Mic 6:8).

Since the Hebrew Bible is so evidently concerned with justice and the care of the vulnerable in the community, could it be that the New Testament focuses on the individual morality we have come to associate with Christianity?

A careful reading of the Gospels, however, will not sustain this interpretation. After all, the Synoptic Gospels (Matthew, Mark, and Luke) emphasize Jesus' proclamation of the reign of God, a situation in which God rules all of society, rather than merely the hearts of a few. And, as described in these Gospels, God's reign is one of inclusion and equality, where social hierarchy is overturned and those who serve most humbly are the most exalted.

Attention to the similarities between the Sermon on the Plain in the Gospel of Luke and the Sermon on the Mount in the Gospel of Matthew further discloses their common interest in a Christian spirituality of social justice. In Luke 6:17–24, we find Jesus promising radical social change in the Sermon on the Plain (so-called because the author of the Gospel of Luke tells us that Jesus came down from a hill and began to preach on level ground). Here, Jesus proclaims that the poor will inherit God's reign, those who are hungry now will be filled, those who are weeping will laugh, and those who are excluded and insulted will be rewarded by God. Jesus also warns that the rich have already had their happiness, those who are well fed will be hungry, and those who are now laughing will weep.

This social reversal appears earlier in the Gospel of Luke, even before Jesus' birth, when his mother, Mary, proclaims God's goodness to her. Mary (echoing Hannah in the Hebrew Bible) announces that God "has brought down the powerful from their thrones, / and lifted up the lowly; / he has filled the hungry with good things, / and sent the rich away empty" (Luke 1:52–53).[3]

Later, in chapter 16 of the Gospel of Luke, Jesus further underscores the coming reversal of fortunes with his story of the poor man, Lazarus, and a rich man who is unnamed. (This is in itself a striking reversal, since it is the poor who are usually anonymous, while the wealthy and powerful are well-known.) In this familiar story, the rich man, who has enjoyed the good things of life, dies and experiences the torment of Hades, while Lazarus, who was starving at the rich man's gate, dies and is taken to be comforted in the afterlife. In an intriguing detail of this story, when the rich man begs for Lazarus to be sent to warn his brothers, Abraham tells the rich man that they have already been warned—by Moses and the prophets. Clearly, the author of this Gospel wants the reader to understand that Jesus considered care for the poor and vulnerable to be an important part of the Mosaic Law (the laws in the Torah) as well as of the prophetic books (see Luke 16:19–31).

When we turn to the Sermon on the Mount in Matthew 5:1–12 (where Jesus preaches from a mountainside), it might seem as though Jesus has shifted away from social concerns and is instead giving "spiritual" advice. In place of Luke's "blessed are you who are poor," we find in Matthew "blessed are the poor in spirit." Similarly, rather than "blessed are you who are hungry," the text of Matthew reads "blessed are those who hunger and thirst for righteousness." The meek and merciful are also praised, as are the pure in heart and the peacemakers.

DIVINE HARMONY

Teachers and preachers often explain that these Beatitudes (so named because they specify who is blessed, or *beatus*) can be read as "be-attitudes": attitudes that ought to characterize one's way of being in the world.

But isn't there quite a shift from Luke's concern with social change to Matthew's focus on internal attitudes? Instead of Luke's vision of a social reversal in which the hungry are fed and the rich become hungry, we have in Matthew's Gospel an emphasis on personal virtues of humility, meekness, and mercy as essential to Christian discipleship.

But to read Matthew and Luke as in conflict here is a mistake. Matthew's Sermon on the Mount is not intended to present a spiritualization of Christianity that would leave societal injustice and inequality in place. Rather, Matthew gives us a description of the attitudes and virtues that Jesus' disciples must cultivate in order to follow him in living the justice and inclusion of God's reign.[4] People who seek justice for the poor must be poor in spirit and meek; that is, they must be willing to depend on God and give up the desire to dominate over others. There is no room for pride or for the lust for power in God's inclusive reign. Further, as people who strive to achieve that new society in which all of the hungry are fed, Jesus' disciples must hunger and thirst for the righteousness, the right-living that establishes justice. They must also be willing to be persecuted in the cause of justice, even while they remain committed to the mercy that makes possible a reconciling peace.

My point here is that the Gospels of Luke and Matthew are not contradicting each other, or even in tension. Rather, they are discussing different aspects of the same hope for God's reign of inclusion and equality. Luke emphasizes the changes in society that will occur when all live according to God's will, whereas Matthew is describing the changes in attitude required of those who wish to live in and for God's coming reign.

Further evidence that the Gospel of Matthew places care for those in need at the heart of Christian spirituality is provided by the parable of the final judgment in Matthew 25:31–43. In this story, which appears only in Matthew's Gospel, Jesus tells his audience that one's ultimate destiny, eternal life or eternal punishment, is determined by whether one feeds the hungry, gives drink to the thirsty, welcomes the stranger into one's house, clothes the naked, cares for the sick, and visits the imprisoned.

Perhaps surprisingly, this passage suggests that whether one believes in or consciously chooses to follow Jesus is irrelevant. Instead, what matters is how one responds to the vulnerable and marginalized. As we are told in Matthew 25:40, the Son of Man so deeply identifies with the people society rejects that he will declare, "Just as you did it to one of the least of these who are members of my family, you did it to me."

These examples indicate that the New Testament shares the Hebrew Bible's attention to constructing a just society, one in which the vulnerable are protected rather than abused. Indeed, we find throughout the Bible, in both Testaments, that commitment to social justice and care for those in need are key spiritual values, central to love of God and neighbor.

CHRISTIAN TRADITION: REDISCOVERING THE SOCIAL GOSPEL

Despite the biblical emphasis on social justice, we must admit that social issues have sometimes been neglected in Christian life (as Gilkey's experience with the church group's rejection of "material" concerns suggests). Especially in recent times, Christian faith has often been understood as a personal matter affecting only one's inner life and afterlife. The result is an individualistic Christianity in which the justice of social institutions and the causes of poverty can be dismissed as irrelevant to Christian love.

Since the late nineteenth century, however, notable Christian leaders (including Pope Leo XIII) have been paying more attention to Christian responsibility for justice in society. It became apparent that the modern world, with its industrialization of the work force and growing separation of rich and poor, posed new challenges for traditional Christian ideas of societal harmony. At the same time, more thinkers were questioning the view that Christianity was concerned only with issues of private life, a perspective that had spread in the post-Enlightenment world. Many felt the need for renewed and sustained thought about the church's relationship to modern society, political democracy, and industrial capitalism.

One of the American leaders of this rekindled interest in the social responsibilities of Christianity was the Baptist minister and theologian Walter Rauschenbusch. During the nineteenth century's "gilded age," when a new American aristocracy based on money was celebrating its excessive wealth, Rauschenbusch was pastoring a congregation of impoverished immigrants in the Hell's Kitchen area of New York City. He was deeply disturbed by the suffering of these poor—and by the rest of society's indifference to them. This experience inspired Rauschenbusch to become a leader of the social gospel movement in the United States, working tirelessly to recover a commitment to social justice in a Christianity preoccupied with individual souls.

Rauschenbusch's gilded age shares much in common with our own time. The late nineteenth century in the United States was marked by great inequality. Indeed, Rauschenbusch himself cited statistics about the enormous wealth of the richest *1 percent* of the population, who then owned more than 50 percent of the nation's total wealth.[5] A similar focus on the disproportionate wealth of the top 1 percent has again become part of our national conversation, popularized by the Occupy Wall Street movement's critique of the recent surge in inequality in America. According to current statistics, inequality in the United States is now at its highest point since the gilded age, with the top 1 percent now owning approximately 35 percent of the nation's wealth.

Many Christians today would also recognize the emphasis on individual sins and personal redemption in the Christianity of

Rauschenbusch's youth, though few are likely to have experienced the exclusive focus on private life that Rauschenbusch reports. The Christianity Rauschenbusch grew up with apparently lacked any awareness that social justice is, or ought to be, a central Christian concern, even in the midst of growing inequality and the immense suffering of the poor, the marginalized, and the vulnerable.

Faced with the dominance of this "privatized" Christianity preoccupied with individual souls, Rauschenbusch realized that people would not be easily convinced that social reform is integral to Christian faith. So he returned to Christianity's authoritative sources, the Bible and the early church, and argued in his influential *Christianity and the Social Crisis* that key elements of each of these sources emphasize social justice. Though he feared he might be fired from his teaching position for so publicly challenging the piety of his day, Rauschenbusch's appeal to the importance of justice in the Hebrew Bible law and prophets, to the centrality of the reign of God in the preaching of Jesus, and to the social values of the early Christian communities, met with sweeping success. His book became a best seller.

Jesus' preaching of the reign of God was particularly important in Rauschenbusch's theology. He found here a theme that was not only central to Jesus' own ministry as portrayed in the New Testament Gospels, but also one that incorporated the various aspects of Christianity that Rauschenbusch valued. Since God's reign begins in history but is fulfilled only beyond history, this reign encompasses life in this world as well as the afterlife. In other words, this world matters—it is where God's reign grows, and not merely a place to test whether one merits heaven, as some theologies have suggested. Yet at the same time, our hope is not tied to or limited by inevitably flawed human projects, since Christians ultimately anticipate a perfected community beyond what is possible in time.

Nor does this emphasis on social justice displace a personal relationship with God, in Rauschenbush's view. To live in God's reign is to accept God's will and intentions for humanity, and this entails the personal submission to God's will that was at the heart of Rauschenbusch's own conversion experience. Believing that sin was both personal and social, Rauschenbusch was committed to an account of God's grace transforming persons as well as society.

His theological work of recovering the role of societal reform in the Bible and the early church was far from Rauschenbusch's only contribution, however. He also analyzed economic and legal structures in order to determine the causes of poverty and to clarify what faith in God's reign required in his day. For example, Rauschenbusch opposed the abuse of workers frequently forced to labor long hours without adequate pay, job security, or safe working conditions, and he critiqued the economic forces that underlay this systemic oppression.

Industrialism could have made life better for all by allowing greater productivity with less labor, Rauschenbusch observed. It did not turn out that way, he argued, because the machines were so expensive that they were not owned by and operated for the benefit of guilds of workers. Instead, the machines were the property of a few who used them to enrich themselves at the expense of their workers. Laborers were forced to accept subsistence wages so that production would be more "efficient," producing greater profits for the owners with less cost for the consumers. (Even though much has changed in our contemporary global capitalist system, the current wage stagnation of workers while profits and CEO salaries soar suggests that Rauschenbusch's analysis may still have some merit today.)

Rauschenbusch recognized that these abuses were systemic problems rather than the personal failures of particularly cruel capitalists. The owners were, after all, under considerable pressure to remain competitive. Without the support of government regulation, any individual factory owner who decided to pay a just wage was likely to be undersold by less scrupulous producers, and thus would end in bankruptcy.

Goodwill alone was clearly not enough. Indeed, Rauschenbusch noted that vast inequality is itself a barrier to human community because, especially as wealth becomes inherited, people no longer share similar circumstances or know others from different classes. Unequal societies are separated not only by wealth and class but also by a profound ignorance of the conditions of others' lives. This division makes a mockery of any claim to social harmony.

For these reasons, Rauschenbusch identified justice as a "social" form of love. As he explained, "The old advice of love breaks down before the hugeness of modern relations....It is indeed love that we want, but it is a socialized love," by which he meant a love expressed in building more just legal and socioeconomic structures that would ultimately benefit all.[6] Rauschenbusch hoped for a democratic socialism with workers owning and operating their factories collectively, but he also supported more moderate reforms that were eventually adopted, such as a minimum wage, a maximum work day with safe working conditions, social security for the sick and elderly, and government standardization of pharmaceuticals.

Rauschenbusch's ideal of democratic socialism has not yet been achieved, at least in the United States, and many of the problems of worker abuse that Rauschenbusch identified have now become the global problems of an international capitalism. Yet Rauschenbusch succeeded far beyond what he had originally expected when he feared he would be fired for the book that he courageously wrote anyway to "discharge a debt" to the men and women who had shared their lives with him.[7] There is perhaps a lesson here for all who feel that what we do and say will make no difference, especially in the face of massive socioeconomic systems.

Rauschenbusch became a celebrated author, but more importantly, the socially engaged Christianity he and others in the social gospel movement advocated became the dominant form of Protestant Christianity in the United States through much of the twentieth century. Mainstream Protestant churches were persuaded that Christian love required justice, and their support for social reform made possible successful legislation (such as Roosevelt's "New Deal") to curb some of the abuses that Rauschenbusch drew attention to.

DIVINE HARMONY

Many Christian theologians and theological movements (including Black, feminist, Latino, liberationist, and public theologies) continue Rauschenbusch's work of analyzing both social structures and the sources of Christian faith to gain insight into what it means to follow Jesus today. However, there is also much to be gained from another significant approach to Christian social responsibility: the publication of church documents about particular social concerns. One particularly influential and well-developed collection of such church writings is known as Catholic social teaching, a collection of significant documents on social issues released by popes, by the Second Vatican Council, and by regional councils of Catholic bishops.

Modern Catholic social teaching began at about the same time as the social gospel movement, with the publication in 1891 of Pope Leo XIII's encyclical On Capital and Labor (or, as it is commonly known, *Rerum Novarum*). Other writings on social issues by popes and bishops followed, contributing to the development of a Catholic perspective on sociopolitical concerns in the modern world. These documents tend to be explanatory rather than argumentative, and are usually rather general in their treatment of the matters in question. It is rare to find in these writings the specificity of social analysis provided by Rauschenbusch and other theologians. The strength of this approach is found instead in its ability to express the consensus of the faith community and to provide general principles to guide Christian sociopolitical action.

The coherence of Catholic social teaching is best grasped in terms of its underlying emphasis on persons-in-community. Indeed, throughout much of the twentieth century (and especially during the Cold War tensions between U.S. capitalism and Soviet communism), Catholic social teaching clearly and deliberately affirmed a persons-in-community approach in opposition to what popes saw then as the two dominant but mistaken options: a Western individualism that neglected community and an Eastern communalism that denied the dignity of the individual. As an alternative to both of these, Catholic social teaching affirmed the dignity and rights of the person along with the importance of the community in which persons become themselves.

Because each human being is of sacred worth simply because s/he exists, regardless of achievement or status, Catholic social teaching maintains that every person has a claim to a share of the community resources that are essential for personal development. This entails the right to the means of a decent life (including adequate food, shelter, and medical care); the right to freedom of conscience, religion, and expression; the right to contribute to society through one's work, along with the right to a living wage and decent work conditions; the right to education and culture; and the right to participate in the decisions that affect one's life and community.

The astute reader will note that Catholic social teaching goes well beyond the U.S. acknowledgment of individual political rights, affirming also the economic rights emphasized in other countries. According to these Catholic documents, recognition of the dignity of each person requires Christians to strive to ensure that all people have the material, educational, and cultural resources they need for full personal development.

Other key principles of Catholic social teaching focus on responsibility to the larger community. One of the most important of these principles insists that political and economic decisions should serve the common good in which all flourish. Instead of "voting our pocketbooks," as the common saying has it, or supporting policies that privilege our own social group or class at the expense of others, Catholic social teaching calls for a politics that seeks the good of all humanity.

Commitment to pursuing this common good requires the political virtue of solidarity with all people, a global solidarity. Christians believe that all members of the human race are created and loved by God, and oriented to an everlasting life together with others in God's reign. A politics that serves the true common good cannot be directed solely to the shared good of one's own class, race, religion, or even nation. The common good must be a global good.

Even while our solidarity and commitment to the common good are properly universal, extended to the whole of humanity, Catholic social teaching gives a privileged place to the option for the poor (including all of the insignificant, the powerless, and the marginalized or excluded, even those who may not be monetarily poor). Remembering God's overwhelming concern for the poor throughout the Bible, those of us who are not poor must pay special attention to those who are most vulnerable and who have the least power and privilege in society.

This option for the poor does not contradict the universality of the common good, as it may seem. If all are to flourish together, it is essential that we ensure the inclusion of those who are most often and most easily ignored. Only through a developed option for the poor—through taking time to consider the perspectives, needs, and circumstances of those whom society considers least—can we hope to make decisions that truly serve the common good of all.

The principle of subsidiarity is another key theme of Catholic social teaching. Subsidiarity seeks to safeguard the right to participation in community life by requiring that decisions be made at the most local level possible. However, the principle of subsidiarity also supports regional, national, and even (potentially) international political authority: in the official Catholic understanding of subsidiarity, higher levels of government have an obligation to become involved when the local community is not able to achieve its goals or resolve its problems on its own. In this world, community depends upon both participation and organized cooperation, with proper authority at all levels.

Given its emphasis on global community, peace is also a major theme in Catholic social teaching. While the possibility of a justified war as an option of last resort is not ruled out, the contemporary emphasis is decidedly on the importance of a thorough and even sacrificial dedication to overcoming conflict and building a lasting peace. Recent teachings have further noted that some current weapons are so indiscriminately destructive that their use cannot be made consistent with an appropriately proportionate use of violence or with the protection due to noncombatants.

Care for creation is the latest principle developed in Catholic social teaching. While stewardship of natural resources for the good of others has been an integral part of the Catholic tradition, the current capacity of humanity to inflict long-term damage on our environment has inspired fresh attention to the value of creation in itself. Nature must be protected not only as essential to human life, but for its own sake—Genesis 1 tells us that God created the world and declared it all to be good. To limit ourselves to concern for humanity is to fail to realize the extent of our relationality, which includes not only relationships with God and with the human community but also with all that God has created and sustains in existence.

In sum, Catholic social thought insists that Christian love must serve both persons and the communities that sustain persons. Social institutions and structures—indeed, all the resources of this earth—should be directed to the good of all of creation, individually and collectively. The community of the church is called to contribute to contemporary society by defending the dignity and rights of each distinct person (especially the poor, vulnerable, and marginalized), while also striving to ensure that socioeconomic and political institutions facilitate the common good, the good of all that is.

Catholic social teaching shares with the Protestant social gospel movement a commitment to social justice as part of the love of neighbor and as integral to the goal of complete harmony in God. Langdon Gilkey's theological mentor, Paul Tillich, provides a particularly helpful explanation of this integral relationship between justice and love. Christians believe, as Tillich notes, that creation is intended by God for a unity that is currently lacking. Love, then, seeks to unite what is now (but should not be) separated. Justice, however, is necessary to preserve what is separated until it can be fully united in love. (Consider, for example, how injustice, such as lack of decent wages, keeps people from flourishing and in too many cases causes premature death.) Love, uniting all in mutuality and harmony, is the ultimate ideal for Christians, but that ideal cannot be achieved without the justice that enables the vulnerable and less powerful to survive.[8]

In the final analysis, what justice has not preserved, love will not be able to unite, and so Christian love requires—and builds on—an active commitment to justice.

LIVING A WITNESS OF LOVE-IN-JUSTICE

As we know all too well, there is no lack of suffering and injustice begging for redress today. In fact, the needs of the world can be truly overwhelming. As Christians, we are called to a universal solidarity that values each person, yet as participants in an increasingly global economy, we are involved in (and many of us benefit from) a system that distributes gains and costs unequally. The slave labor of young women in China, for example, enables North Americans to indulge the desire for ever new and more stylish clothes. Consumption of fossil fuels is causing global warming and resulting in a sea level rise that is already devastating island nations.

In this multifaceted and interconnected reality, there can be no simple or uniform prescription for how to live a life that contributes to a world of greater justice informed by, and oriented to, love. Differing talents, opportunities, and personal concerns inspire varying responses to the many problems and injustices of this world. It has been wisely said that a person's true vocation is found at the point where that person's deepest passions coincide with the world's greatest needs.

Perhaps the best general advice for Christians committed to living a more just and loving life comes from the current pope, Francis. Refusing to separate spiritual and material needs as Gilkey's audience once did, Pope Francis calls every Christian to a life of prayer and of active concern for the poor (*Evangelii Gaudium* 3, 201).[9]

Most Christians recognize that prayer of some kind is integral to Christian life. In prayer, we overcome our self-centeredness and open ourselves to that greater unity with God that empowers, and is expressed in, unity with all else that God loves into being.

Not all Christians, however, accept that each of us must be personally involved with the poor and the marginalized. Even though Pope Francis declares that "no one must say that they cannot be close to the poor," the reality is that many of us do consider ourselves so important that we "outsource" the option for the poor, leaving to others the difficult and time-consuming task of building solidarity with those society considers of little value (*Evangelii Gaudium* 201).[10] Yet when the majority of the human race (and of nature) is treated as disposable, how can a commitment to God's inclusive and loving reign be real if it is not expressed in active resistance to this devaluing of people and nature?

The martyred Archbishop of San Salvador, Blessed Oscar Romero, provides a powerful example of a life of prayer lived in dedication to the poor. In his life and in his death, Romero witnessed to the inseparability of prayer, especially the Eucharistic Prayer, and a prophetic commitment to seeking justice for the impoverished, oppressed, and politically abused in his country.[11]

It is not surprising to find a bishop associated with prayer. After all, a major part of the bishop's role in the early church was to preside over the weekly gathering for worship. Still today, bishops are understood in many Christian traditions as powerful symbols of the church when they preside over the eucharistic worship celebrating the unity of the people with God and with each other in the Body of Christ.

There have also, of course, been bishops throughout the church's history that demanded justice for the poor (though not perhaps as many as might be hoped). But Archbishop Romero is an extraordinary example of how eucharistic worship and defense of the poor can be integrally related. For example, when people were unable to learn the names and fate of those who had "disappeared" in police custody, Romero adopted the practice of including this information in his Sunday homily, which was broadcast over the diocesan radio. Romero thus resisted the brutality of the government while at the same time presiding over the central prayer of the church, thus inserting the disappeared and those mourning for them into the heart of the ecclesial community.

A formative event in Romero's early tenure as archbishop encouraged this explicit link between justice and the eucharistic worship of the diocese. To protest and to mourn the government's assassination of one of his priests, Fr. Rutilio Grande, Archbishop Romero invited all Catholics to come to (or listen to the broadcast of) the Sunday liturgy at the cathedral. All other Masses throughout the diocese at that time were cancelled. The people gathered together in a profound expression of unity as the whole diocese liturgically celebrated the life and mourned the death of this priest who had dedicated himself to the poor.

Romero died as he lived: presiding over the Eucharist and working for justice in his country. The day before he died, during his Sunday homily, Romero again challenged the government's brutal repression of the poor. He called on soldiers to refuse to fire on civilians, even when ordered to do so. Romero was assassinated the next day, while saying Mass.

An important part of Romero's story is that the integral relation of justice and eucharistic prayer so evident in his later life and death was not always apparent to him. In his younger years, he struggled with the teachings of the Second Vatican Council on social engagement. At that time, Romero feared that too much emphasis on social justice would detract from the peace and reconciliation promised by the Gospel. Perhaps he was not too different from the churchwoman at the beginning of this chapter, who did not want to distract from spiritual values by attending to material needs. Yet

Romero was a man of prayer, and as his openness to God and his love for his people grew, he came to know the depth of their suffering. He realized that the gospel's promise of peace and reconciliation could only be built on a foundation of loving justice.

Recognizing that God is not glorified while God's poor are oppressed, Romero lived and died a faithful witness to the impossibility of separating prayerful praise of God and work for greater justice. Romero's life and death also serve as a reminder that a love that does justice is neither easy nor risk free. But then, of course, it wasn't risk free for Jesus either.

Chapter 5

GLOBAL COMMUNITY

VULNERABILITY AND HOSPITALITY

FROM ITS EARLIEST DAYS, Christianity has recognized a responsibility to foster universal solidarity. It could not be otherwise, since an authentic Christian understanding of persons-in-community ultimately encompasses the whole world, in a community without limits.

In our increasingly global age, this universal solidarity is crucial since humanity is profoundly—but by no means always positively—interconnected. One of the greatest questions we face today is: What kind of globalization will we develop? Will our interactions serve all, or will the benefits go, as so often, to the few? Will we come together in cooperation and community, or in competition and conflict?

The urgent need for active solidarity and mutual support is particularly clear in the heartbreaking tragedy of Alan Kurdi, a Syrian child whose drowned body washed up on a beach in Turkey in early September 2015. Determined to escape the ongoing violence in Syria and unable to obtain the documents that would allow them to join relatives in Canada, the Kurdi family risked crossing the rough sea in a rubber raft in hopes of getting into Europe. The boat flipped in the turbulent water, and three-year-old Alan, his five-year-old brother Ghalib, and their mother, Rehan, drowned.[1]

The world would not have noticed the deaths of these few refugees, had it not been for the photo of Alan's body lying on the beach the next morning. In the picture, Alan seemed to be asleep, napping with the innocence of a child who, of course, had no responsibility for the war, violence, bureaucratic immigration policies, and unsafe boat that led to his death. One small, precious boy was lost because he was caught up in geopolitical forces from which no one rescued him.

The photo of little Alan personalized the tragedy of the many refugees around the world who are desperately trying to escape violent and inhuman situations. Indifference and even hostility toward Syrian refugees was interrupted (at least partially and temporarily) by the sad picture of Alan. Instead of the feared waves of refugees flooding their countries, Europeans and Americans saw a little child drowned in the sea because too few cared enough to ensure that he and his family were welcomed into a secure and stable community.

But human history reminds us how difficult it can be for people to live together in harmony, especially members of different groups. Violence, oppression, and colonization often mark the encounter between human communities. And indeed, just a few months after the death of Alan touched hearts around the world, Syrian refugees (including children) were again seen primarily as threats to be guarded against rather than as vulnerable people to be welcomed. Many Europeans became preoccupied with protecting their culture and economy, while politicians in the United States stoked fear that ISIS terrorists might sneak into the country among the Syrian refugees fleeing those very terrorists. Regret for the death of Alan was forgotten as defending the boundaries of established communities became the dominant concern.

Of course, communities do indeed deserve to be nurtured and protected. After all, real community happens in the face-to-face interactions with people we actually encounter in our daily life; universal solidarity can be a rather abstract ideal lacking the concrete demands, blessings, and general messiness of community life.

Moreover, local communities with their distinctness are an integral part of the rich global harmony Christians hope for. As we saw in chapter 2, the ideal of persons-in-community is not a uniformity, but a unity-in-diversity that brings together people with differences, including the different cultural practices and perspectives of distinct communities.

The goal of Christian solidarity is not, then, the "McDonaldization" that homogenizes the world and undermines local cultures. But at the same time, those who affirm the Christian ideal of persons-in-community must also resist the "tribalism" that arises to defend one's community at the expense of other peoples and communities. True diversity cannot be achieved through a defensiveness that pits each group against others.

But what, then, might it mean in our globally interconnected world to seek to live as Christians committed to a universal harmony that nurtures (rather than stifles) local community and cultural diversity? Is an enriching diversity possible in a global age? If so, how might Christianity guide our efforts to cultivate the communities that sustain us without, at the same time, turning our backs on the world's sixty million refugees, over half of whom are children?

THE BIBLE: COMMUNITY AND HOSPITALITY

The Bible has a great deal to say about community distinctness and openness. As is well-known, the identity of the Jewish people has been developed in dialogue with the many stories, detailed law codes, and various other texts of the Hebrew Bible. One of the most important of these is the biblical story of God's covenant with Abraham and with his descendants through Jacob.

DIVINE HARMONY

For no reason (or at least for no reason that we are told in Genesis 12), God makes a covenant with Abraham. He asks Abraham to leave his home in Haran, in present day Syria, and to travel to a new land, promising Abraham, "I will make of you a great nation, and I will bless you, and make your name great, so that you will be a blessing. I will bless those who bless you, and the one who curses you I will curse; and in you all the families of the earth shall be blessed" (Gen 12:2–3). Later, in Genesis 17, God promises that this covenant will be extended to Abraham's descendants, so that they will become a great nation, will be blessed, and will be given the land to which God leads Abraham.

This covenantal identity is a very particular one. It is given to some and not to others, and much of the Book of Genesis is devoted to the story of who inherits the covenant. The covenant is passed to Abraham's son Isaac, but not to his son Ishmael, and to Isaac's son Jacob, but not to Jacob's twin brother Esau. Finally, all twelve sons of Jacob/Israel, who become known as the fathers of the twelve tribes of Israel, are all included in the covenant.

Ishmael and Esau are not forgotten by God: they are blessed in other ways. Ishmael is also promised a great nation of descendants, while Esau prospers and becomes the ancestor of the Edomites. But they are not part of the covenant that determines the identity of the children of Israel.

Although this covenant is specifically between God and (some of) Abraham's descendants, nevertheless the covenant seems to serve some universal purpose. In Genesis 12, as noted above, God not only promises to bless Abraham but also promises that all people will somehow be blessed because of this covenant between God and Abraham.

It is also significant to the story that Abraham is an immigrant with firsthand experience of the dangers of traveling through the desert and of being a foreigner in a new land. After all, he leaves his home to travel to Canaan, and then leaves Canaan for Egypt when Canaan experiences a severe drought. Later, when back in Canaan,

Abraham sees three travelers and the story tells us that, without being asked, Abraham immediately gets up, orders food and drink, and begs the travelers to stop and take refreshment with him. One can assume that Abraham remembers the difficulties of travel and so anticipates how welcome food and drink will be to these strangers.

This hospitality becomes central to Abraham's story and to the covenant, as these three strangers announce that Sarah will give birth to a son (Isaac) within a year. Abraham's generosity is rewarded with the promise of a long-desired child, the son who will inherit the covenant and pass it on to one of his sons and then to his grandsons.

This pattern of learning how to treat foreigners through one's own experience of being vulnerable in a foreign land is repeated in the Hebrew Bible. In the law code by which they are to live in Canaan, God repeatedly tells the people of Israel that any foreigners who live among them are to be treated well. Instead of taking advantage of the vulnerability of strangers, the Israelites must remember their time in Egypt and so respond to any immigrants or sojourners as they would have wanted the Egyptians to respond to them.[2] Exodus 22:21 states, "You shall not wrong or oppress a resident alien, for you were aliens in the land of Egypt." Leviticus 19:33–34 similarly proclaims, "When an alien resides with you in your land, you shall not oppress the alien. The alien who resides with you shall be to you as the citizen among you; you shall love the alien as yourself, for you were aliens in the land of Egypt: I am the LORD your God."

Not unlike Americans who recount their own family stories of migration as a reason to welcome new immigrants, the Hebrew Bible reminds the Jewish people of their history as a migrant people.

There is, of course, also considerable attention to the preservation of group identity in the Hebrew Bible. These are the chosen people who inherit Abraham's covenant with God as well as the responsibility to live by the laws they've been given. Moreover, the Hebrew people are directed to preserve their distinctness from the other peoples around them, not only by their particular religious festivals and forms of worship but also by such markers of difference as male circumcision and dietary regulations. Yet this concern for their religio-ethnic identity does not allow them to be hostile toward any others who travel through their area or who have come to live among them. Instead, the law's codes depict as central to the Jewish people's own religious identity the task of extending care to outsiders in memory of their own ancestors' vulnerability. Welcoming foreigners is, in this case, to be an expression of—rather than a threat to—their own communal identity.

The New Testament continues to affirm this obligation to extend hospitality to the stranger in need. This is especially clear in Jesus' parable of the Good Samaritan told in the Gospel of Luke (10:25–39). The hero of the story is a member of the Samaritan community who comes to the aid of the beaten and robbed Jew, a man who is a stranger to the Samaritan and, worse, a member of a people who are hostile to the Samaritans. The Samaritan saves the life of this unknown enemy after the religious leaders of the victim's own, Jewish, community pass by without helping him.

The behavior of the Samaritan, who gave both time and money to care for an enemy in need, is the model that Jesus gives us in the Gospel of Luke for what it means to fulfill the requirement to love one's neighbor as another self. The neighbors we are commanded to love are not then only the members of our own family or community, those we are bound to by a shared history and mutual care. As the story of the Good Samaritan indicates, the neighbor is instead anyone we encounter who is in need. In other words, to fulfill the command to love our neighbor as ourselves requires that we extend care to those beyond our circle of friendship and community.

This teaching that one must love anyone in need as one's own self is daunting, and clearly in opposition to the tribalism that defends one's own group at the expense of others. Moreover, by making the Samaritan the good figure here, Jesus further questions tribal assumptions that people commonly (if often unconsciously) hold about the moral superiority of their own community. Because the hero of the story is a generous and compassionate Samaritan, Jesus forces his audience to identify with the Samaritan and to relinquish the assumptions that reinforced their hostility toward the Samaritan people.

The force of Jesus' point here is easy to miss for those who have no history of prejudice against Samaritans. I suspect this story needs to be revised from time to time with the identity of the Samaritan changed to whatever group of people (there's always one!) is particularly maligned or despised by the audience. Dare we imagine that, if Jesus were to preach this parable in the United States today, it might be an Arab Muslim who stops to aid a European American Christian ignored by other white Christians.

Of course, the New Testament rejection of tribalism is not limited to the parable of the Good Samaritan, however powerful this story is. After all, Jesus' disciples are given a universal mission, sent to take this message to the whole world and to "make disciples of all nations" (Matt 28:19). All of humanity is to be invited into the covenant between God and humanity through Jesus.

Still, and notwithstanding the global emphasis of the early Christians who travel far to make converts and who welcome gentiles into their movement, the Christian communities they establish have their own significant distinctness. Though the mission of the church is universal, Christians are expected to adopt specific beliefs and practices, including being baptized in the name of the Trinity and following Jesus' teachings. In addition, the Acts of the Apostles depicts the church in Jerusalem as a community of mutual care and responsibility, with new members selling their surplus possessions and land to ensure that all in the community have what they need. The members of this new movement are described as sharing a special bond and as striving to model what true community on earth might be by their care for each other—even if, as Acts and Paul's letters honestly admit, these early Christians do at times fall short of the ideal of care across ethnic and class boundaries.

Indeed, the texts describing the early church suggest that universality and particularity are key aspects of the Christian movement. Jesus' followers know they are sent to bring their very particular hope in Jesus' resurrection to all the world, while living the love that requires them to place God above all and to respond to anyone in need as another self.

Perhaps this is evident in the New Testament's (Greek) word for the church, *ekklesia*, which means "called out." To join the church means that one is joining a specific group, a people called out from the normal patterns of life in society to live God's reign with audacious love and hope. Yet at the same time, *ekklesia* is the word for a public assembly, not a private or exclusive group. The church is to be public in its presence in society and its openness to all, even while the church must not be simply a replication of society. Christianity, while being universal in its inclusivity, remains a distinct community with specific practices and beliefs based in the Scriptures and in hope in the God of Jesus Christ.

CHRISTIAN TRADITION: SEEKING A GLOBAL UNITY-IN-DIVERSITY

Jesus' followers took seriously their commission to go out to all the world as they spread Christianity throughout the Roman Empire and beyond. The young church rapidly became transnational, with thriving communities in many countries. Despite the considerable challenges of travel and communication in the ancient world, these communities, or churches, maintained a sense of unity through visits, letters, prayers for one another, and sending their bishops to participate in the consecration of each other's new bishop. (Of course, it follows that, when divergence in practice or belief was so serious that the communities could no longer recognize each other as members of the same faith, they could—and did—express their disunity by cutting off these practices of mutual recognition.)

Global Community

Even though complete unity among Christians has never been achieved, such union has been an important and deeply valued goal, all the more so because of the implications of the celebration of the Eucharist, or the Lord's Supper. Sharing together in the sacred bread and wine, the participants are together the one Body of Christ, in union with God as well as with all others in God. This communion encompasses not only those immediately present, of course, but also all others in the Body of Christ, which knows no spatial limits.

Since each local church community is part of this global community of churches, the church has rightly been called a "communion of communions." Just as Christians do not properly understand themselves as separate, autonomous individuals but rather as members of a community that enables each to be fully the unique person that he or she is, so also each local church is not separate but is an integral and distinct part of the one Body of Christ. We are not merely persons-in-community, but rather persons-in-communities-in communities (and so on), with each level recognized as valuable both in itself and as a contribution to the greater whole.

Further reflection on the experience of the church, especially as informed by the celebration of the Lord's Supper, has led to a growing agreement among Orthodox, Catholic, and many Protestant Christians about the purpose of the church. This emerging consensus holds that the church's mission in history is twofold. The first part of its task is simply to be a harmonious community united in love of God and each other as a compelling witness to a divided world of the unity that humanity was made for. The second part of the church's task is to work to increase the unity (and decrease the division) of the world. In the words of the Catholic Church's Second Vatican Council (which drew here on the rich theological tradition of the Orthodox churches), the church is called to be a "sign and instrument both of a very closely knit union with God and of the unity of the whole human race" (*Lumen Gentium* 1).[3]

In the half century since the Second Vatican Council, this general understanding of the mission of the church has been affirmed not only by Catholic and Orthodox theologians but also by many Protestant churches and even in recent documents of the World Council of Churches. Although Christians still disagree about many topics concerning the nature of the church and its proper structures of authority, there is nevertheless considerable agreement that the church's purpose is not merely to increase its numbers. Christians of various denominations are increasingly coming to agree that the church is called to be distinct as a loving and united community while, at the same time, the church is meant to serve the whole world as an instrument in God's plan to overcome the world's disharmony. "Communion...is both the gift by which the Church lives and, at the same time, the gift that God calls the Church to offer to a wounded and divided humanity."[4]

Considering the church's mission to be a witness to loving unity, the divisions among Christians are a deep scandal. The ecumenical movement to overcome Christian disunity is not motivated merely by a sense that it would be good if Christians all got along. Instead, work in ecumenism is inspired by the recognition that church divisions are a clear and institutionalized reminder of the church's failure in its mission. A divided church is not a very good witness of the unity God desires, nor can a church that is unable to overcome its own divisions be a very credible or successful instrument of unity in the world.

Of course, it is not to be expected that the church, comprised of fallible and sinful human beings, would fulfill its mission perfectly. Christians can and must hope that God will enable our imperfect efforts to bear fruit despite our failings.

Besides, it is important to keep in mind that the failures in church unity (however glaring) are not the whole story. Perhaps, given the difficulties of humanity, we should be surprised by the church's success in achieving the unity it has rather than dismayed by the church's divisions. After all, Christian communities continue to form national and international networks that strengthen Christian unity and mutual support across cultural, linguistic, ethnic, and national boundaries. The Catholic Church, for example, has a global structure of governance uniting Catholic Christians throughout the world. Many other international denominational and interdenominational organizations also foster common action by Christians of different nationalities and ethnicities, encouraging them to understand themselves as part of a common faith and a single church.

This international Christian unity has been profoundly expressed in the "border Eucharists" held recently in the United States. Congregations, gathered on both sides of the international border between the United States and Mexico, pray together and share the sacred bread that unites us in Christ.[5] When possible, hands are clasped and peace passed through the fence, witnessing against the division the border reinforces. All present are reminded that, despite our tendencies to see each other as enemies, foreigners, and threats to one another's identity, we are one Body of Christ, brothers and sisters, children of the one God.

Nor is this unity limited to those within the Christian tradition, a point that perhaps border Eucharists alone cannot clearly convey. The church, after all, is called to work for the greater unity of all. The Eucharist that celebrates our union with God joins us, then, not only with all other partakers of the Eucharist, but also with all who are united in God's love—in other words, with the entire world.

Despite its (often glaring) failures and imperfections, the church has an ancient tradition of peacemaking, and of extending hospitality to strangers and those in need. Christian hospitals were founded to care for the sick, monasteries have welcomed travelers and those in duress, and many courageous saints (known and unknown) have spent their lives seeking to be peacemakers. Christian organizations around the world continue to provide aid to refugees, as well as food, shelter, medical care, and sometimes simply companionship to those who, for whatever reason and of whatever religious or ethnic background, lack sufficient material, emotional, or spiritual support.

To foster this hospitality to the stranger, Christian traditions include various stories of people unknowingly welcoming Christ in the person of a stranger in need. One of the most beloved of these stories is that of St. Christopher, who sought to serve God by carrying people across a dangerous river. One day he agreed to carry a child across the river and, as they progressed, the child became heavier and heavier. St. Christopher learned that he was carrying the Christ Child and was helping him to bear the sins of the world. It is for this reason that he is called Christopher, or "Christ-bearer," and is honored as the special protector of travelers.

Like St. Christopher, the Good Samaritan, Abraham, and the people of Israel, the church is called to respond with a welcoming, generous hospitality to all in need, especially to those strangers who lack the supportive community that sustains life and enables growth. Affirming (sometimes despite apparent evidence to the contrary) that the world was made for harmony and that human beings become their full selves only in community, the church has been given the mission to unite all in God. The church is thus committed to increasing unity-in-diversity not only among Christians but throughout the whole world.

COMPETITION OR COMMUNITY? A GLOBAL CHALLENGE

We are living through one of the great periods of human migration. Wars, internal violence, persecution, climate change, and the fluctuations of the global economy are causing huge numbers of refugees and other migrants to seek a better life elsewhere. Christians, who have been called to increase unity, must then ask themselves what it means to build community in a world of shifting populations and with so many people bereft of community ties or support.

The reality of the current world situation is that, instead of seeking ways to extend hospitality, anti-immigration forces in

Europe resist admitting refugees, and many of these refugees are dying. At the same time, Americans advocate barriers that increase the deaths (now about 350 per year) of people struggling to cross the Mexico–United States border to escape violence and poverty in their home countries. In a world with so much instability, and with people finding their own comfort and security threatened, it is not surprising that fear so often trumps compassion.

There are, unfortunately, always risks in welcoming a stranger. Do we imagine that Abraham could welcome a group of travelers without any risk to himself or to others in his camp? Or that a Good Samaritan in biblical times would be taking no chances in stopping to aid someone whose appearance of being near death might, after all, be a ruse?

The reality is that welcome of the other is not possible without some willingness to be vulnerable. There is often danger to one's self and one's community: in our current world of sin, crime, and violence, other people can and sometimes are a real threat to our security. Additionally, new people nearly always endanger one's own place in the community, which must reconfigure itself to make room for the new members. The fear that, if we make room for others, they in turn may take over and push us out is a very old fear, and not without some basis in human experience (though it ought to give us pause when we consider that this was the rationale mentioned in Exodus 1 for the enslavement of the Hebrew people).

It would seem to make little sense for the dominant and privileged in a community to risk the displacement that may come with welcoming others, especially if those others are to be extended hospitality such that the guest is no longer a guest but truly at home. That is, it makes little sense unless we realize that we belong to each other, have a common destiny, and are not complete without one another. Then we will recognize there is risk not only in welcoming but also in rejecting immigrants and refugees. If we refuse to open our communities in hospitality to those in need, we cannot become our full selves, our communities cannot grow as they should, and Christians will have failed in their mission to increase human unity.

Perhaps the most important and the most difficult challenge for Christian communities lies not in working to liberalize national immigration policies, but rather in striving to ensure that immigrants are fully welcomed into our churches. The true hospitality expected of a people committed to unity-in-diversity surely requires not merely that new people be allowed to join but that room is made for the diverse languages and cultural practices they bring.

The church, of all places, ought not to insist on the homogenization that welcomes only those willing to adopt the culture and language of the dominant population. Nor has true community been established when different ethnic groups function as separate communities within the same building. When some of our public schools take the time to run bilingual PTA meetings, surely our churches can, at least occasionally, expend the effort to have bilingual worship services, parish meetings, and even social events in which all gather as one community. If we truly believe we belong to one another, how could we *not* take the time to build a common community and to celebrate the distinct gifts each brings to our common life?

The early church affirmed the ideal of all members united as equals without regard for religio-cultural, class, and gender differences in the Christian community. As St. Paul wrote, "There is no longer Jew or Greek, there is no longer slave or free, there is no longer male and female; for all of you are one in Christ Jesus" (Gal 3:28). So also today our churches must give witness to a Christian community that incorporates all as equal members of the Body of Christ. If we are to be united in our diversity, then each church must find ways of integrating ethnic, cultural, and linguistic differences into a new harmony and a greater unity that treats none as second-class citizens.

Accepting that sustaining community means continual change amid the growth and flux of membership, churches that extend a true hospitality to all provide an important witness of the beauty and joy of unity-in-diversity. If religious communities do our part, our fractured and fearful world might yet learn how to extend a more consistent hospitality to one another, and to imagine and enact a globalization that shares the world's resources for the good of all, rather than the enrichment of a few.

Chapter 6

THE GIFT OF TRADITION

MEMORY AND HOPE

LIKE MANY–PROBABLY MOST–Americans, I grew up valuing personal freedom and admiring the self-made, self-reliant individual. "Tradition" struck me as something entirely negative, even though I was raised (and remain) a Catholic, a member of a tradition-embracing form of Christianity. Like most of my peers during my youth, I was suspicious of any claim for the authority of the past. We considered tradition oppressive, "the hand of the dead on the throats of the living," as someone once described it.

This inability to recognize the positive role of tradition was at odds with my actual experience of Catholicism as warm, nurturing, and flexible in the wisdom of its long tradition. I knew that the religious sisters in my grade school (who were semicloistered and still wore their habits of veils and black dresses) were steeped in tradition. I also knew that they had uncommonly large hearts, great patience, and broad perspectives. These women were anything but rigid.

In college, I encountered the Jesuit order of priests, and came to know men whose formation in a centuries-old spirituality gave them greater depth, and more flexibility, than most other people I knew.

Nevertheless, these experiences did not immediately cause me to rethink my rejection of tradition. I had no conceptual framework to help me understand that tradition had formed these women and men to live their generous, vibrant, and creative lives.

Instead, I continued to think of tradition as clinging to outdated customs. I didn't realize that tradition is much more than a repetition of centuries-old practices like the Latin Mass or the full habits of nuns—forms that, despite their longevity, arose at particular times and may not be appropriate in another time or context. More important than any of these particular traditions that come and go over the course of Christian history is the essential function of tradition: it represents the development of a community's wisdom through time.

The rejection of tradition continues to dominate American culture. The history of our communities or the insights of our elders are seldom consulted. Instead, people are fixated on the latest technological innovations. Rather than valuing the past, we download the newest apps for our cell phones and try to keep up with the most popular social media so that we aren't left behind.

To be sure, society experiences waves of traditionalist nostalgia. But these appeals to "tradition" usually neglect tradition as a communal and developing reality. Instead, nostalgic traditionalism seeks to revive the perspectives and practices of specific moments of the past without attention to their historical context. The result is often a pastiche of practices from different times, forced on the present with an inflexibility that ignores tradition as a living, growing reality.

Perhaps more to the point, this nostalgic traditionalism is every bit as individualistic in its own way as is the rejection of tradition. In fact, these are usually the other sides of the same coin: both approaches attempt to invent a pattern of life apart from the wisdom of an ongoing, shared tradition. The antitradition side of the coin fails to recognize that tradition can embody the collective insights developed by a community over considerable time. The nostalgic, supposedly protradition, side claims to honor the author-ity of the past, yet these "traditionalists" choose for themselves as they sift through past options without benefit of the wisdom and guidance of a broader community. Neither side appreciates the value of being part of a living, developing tradition, one carried by a community that extends through time as it forms, and is formed by, new members.

Despite their apparent differences, then, both of these seemingly opposite approaches—antitraditionalism and nostalgic traditionalism—are individualistic, ahistorical, and ultimately blind to the value and richness of tradition. As such, they reinforce rather than resist contemporary American society's focus on the present moment, the "eternal now" in which consumers are preoccupied with the latest new product or fad. Without a sense of belonging to a community that continues through time, it is difficult to withstand our culture's emphasis on the immediate present and its marketing of ever-new products to consume—right now! The desires of the moment are all that seem to matter.

Bombarded by marketing campaigns promoting instant grati-fication, people bereft of a sustaining tradition are also ill equipped to deal with problems that require a longer perspective or a deeper wisdom. Consumer capitalism encourages us to think and to act as individuals who live only for the moment, making consumer choices that will give us the most personal pleasure or best express our individuality. As our political discussions show only too well, any issue that requires attention to historical context or communal obli-gation—or cannot be solved through marketing a new product—receives little sustained public attention.

Yet this ahistorical individualism does not—and cannot—fulfill even its promise to provide an authentic, personal sense of meaning. It fails in this not only because consumerism is ultimately unsatisfying (no matter how many products we can choose among), but also because living solely for the present moment undercuts any sense of meaning beyond our finite lives.

After all, if the past is irrelevant to the present, then it follows that we, in our turn, will be just as irrelevant to the future. How much then can our lives truly matter? If each life occurs as an isolated, more-or-less self-determined moment, what meaning is left when our moment is over?

After a youth of antitraditionalism, I eventually grew to understand that my rejection of tradition meant denying the depth of my connection to others in the past and in the future. The Christian view of persons-in-community, on the other hand, teaches us that the communities that form us extend not only through space (as discussed in the previous chapter) but also through time. We inherit a debt from those who came before us, a debt that is repaid in what we pass on to those who will come after.

At its best, tradition is not a mindless repetition of past practices, but rather an invitation to participate in a community that interrupts our individualism with a hope that encompasses previous as well as future generations.

THE BIBLE: A TRADITION OF MEMORY AND HOPE

The Bible is, of course, deeply concerned with tradition, specifically with developing a communal tradition that remembers a people's encounters with God. The writings collected in the Bible, including stories, laws, prayers, poetry, and visions, have been passed down so that later generations can understand their own experiences of God in relation to, and as part of, this community and its tradition.

Among the many stories of the Hebrew Bible, the Exodus story of God's intervention to free the Hebrew people from slavery in Egypt stands out for its importance to the Jewish community. An account of this liberation from slavery is retold yearly in the Jewish celebration of Passover, as commanded in Exodus 12 as well as in several other places in the Hebrew Bible.

This story is so important that the laws set forth in the Book of Exodus begin with the reminder that the Exodus is central to the community's relationship to God. As a prelude to the laws, we find the statement, "I am the Lord your God, who brought you out of the land of Egypt, out of the house of slavery" (Exod 20:2). The laws that follow, including those we call "the Ten Commandments," are not then presented as laws for all of humanity, however broadly applicable the prohibitions of stealing, murder, lying, and adultery may be. Instead, these commandments are addressed to a specific people who receive these laws as part of their relationship to God, their liberator.

We might well ask what difference it makes that a memory of having been slaves, an oppressed people freed by God, is central to a community's identity. As we have seen in our previous discussion of the biblical law codes, the story of their own past enslavement is integral to the Jewish obligation to care for the vulnerable. The laws remind the people again and again that their ancestors were enslaved and abused as strangers in a foreign land, and on this basis, they are forbidden to oppress strangers in their land.

Perhaps more to our purposes here, though, is this question: What does it mean to affirm that this story of liberated slaves is also Sacred Scripture for Christians? Even though few Christians today claim biological descent from the ancient Hebrews, the Exodus narrative is nevertheless held by Christians to be a revelation of God and part of the Christian faith. Christians learn here that God acts in history to free the oppressed and to protect the vulnerable, and that God calls us to do the same.

There is a temptation to read the story of the Exodus as though God is only concerned with the freedom of God's "chosen" people. Any such limitation of God's compassion ignores the various places (in the law codes and in the prophetic books) in which God commands the people to extend to the vulnerable and the stranger the care that God has shown them. Passages such as "If you do not oppress the alien, the orphan, and the widow, or shed innocent blood...then I will dwell with you in this place" challenge any claim that God cares only for the well-being of the Jewish (or Christian) people (Jer 7:6–7).[1] The broader tradition of the Hebrew Bible affirms God's concern for all the vulnerable and oppressed.

Another significant element in the tradition formed by the Hebrew Bible is the attention the prophets give to Israel's violation of its covenant with God. American Christians, who tend to prefer an idealized version of their nation's history, can easily miss the point of remembering these prophetic condemnations. The important thing is not that the ancient Israelites were extraordinarily unjust to the poor or unusually unfaithful to God; after all, an honest review of Christian history would surely conclude that Christians have been no better. Injustice to the poor, failure to care for the vulnerable, and a strong inclination to value wealth, status, and money more than God have certainly been common in Christian history. The prophets' criticisms are to be remembered not because they demonstrate that the Jews have been particularly unfaithful, but rather because they remind us of God's fidelity and compassion for the poor. God continues throughout history to defend the oppressed and to remind the people of their responsibilities to those in need.

This ancient Jewish tradition of remembering past failures ought to inspire Christians to face our own history, with its failures and sins, more honestly. Rather than justifying a self-righteous superiority (as though Christians never fail in love of God or neighbor!), the prophetic books invite us to hope in a God of endless compassion rather than in our own all-too-human efforts.

One more point about the prophetic tradition should be mentioned here, and this is the role the prophets play in developing the Jewish tradition. By proclaiming that worship is of no value when the people fail to care for the poor and vulnerable (as we see, for example, in Isa 1; Amos 5; and Jer 6), the prophets refine the people's understanding of God and of God's will. Similarly, in their visions of a future harmony, the prophets contribute to the growth of Jewish hope for a time of complete peace and justice.

In other words, the tradition doesn't end with the giving of the laws, as important as the laws are. The prophetic books are also essential in shaping this tradition's understanding of God's will in history.

While Christians embrace the heritage of the Hebrew Bible, Christianity's central memory (as the four Gospels make clear) is not the Exodus but the life, death, and resurrection of Jesus of Nazareth. The New Testament Gospels, in their different approaches and styles, tell the story of Jesus as a Jewish teacher who proclaims God's reign; is crucified by the Roman governor, Pontius Pilate; and is experienced by his followers as resurrected from the dead. It is here, in the life and person of this Jesus, that Christians find God to be most fully revealed.

These stories of Jesus' life and teachings are themselves, of course, a way of interpreting or remembering the traditions of the Hebrew Bible. Jesus, as described in the Gospels, is steeped in the Jewish tradition and stands with the prophets in emphasizing the priority of justice and compassion over ritual obligation. The Gospel of Matthew, for example, includes incidents in which Jesus reminds religious authorities that God desires mercy rather than sacrifice, as declared by the prophet Hosea (see Hos 6:6; Matt 9:13; 12:7). The Gospel of Luke similarly depicts Jesus taking the side of those oppressed by strict religious rules, with Jesus sharply criticizing the authorities that "load people with burdens hard to bear" (Luke 11:46).

Jesus' life and ministry as presented in the Synoptic Gospels is focused on the Jewish hope for the coming of God's reign, that time when God's will for harmony will be fully realized. As the Gospel of Mark particularly emphasizes, Jesus proclaims that the fulfillment of this ancient hope is about to begin at last. According to this Gospel, Jesus begins his public ministry by declaring, "The time is fulfilled, and the kingdom of God has come near" (Mark 1:15). Jesus then summons people to be part of this kingdom, to join him in living now according to the values of God rather than by the values of the powerful who currently rule this world.

In his actions as well as in his teaching, Jesus demonstrates his commitment to God's reign as inclusive of the marginalized, and as valuing those whom the world deems irrelevant. Of course, Jesus does not reject wealthy and important people—the rich man in the Synoptic Gospel accounts is invited to give up his wealth and privilege and join Jesus' community (see Matt 19:16–30; Mark 10:17–23; Luke 18:18–30). However, Jesus' focus is not primarily on those with money and power (who are the center of the world's attention), but rather on the poor and the outcast, including sex workers and others who do not meet the requirements for social respectability. Those who are forced to the margins of society are at the center of the community Jesus gathered, and this scandalizes the religious authorities who demand to know why Jesus demeans himself by eating with tax collectors and sinners (see, e.g., Matt 9:10; Mark 2:16; Luke 5:30; 7:34; 15:1–2).

Challenging social norms or questioning the privileges of the powerful are seldom ways of winning friends in high places, as Jesus would have known. It is surely no surprise to Jesus that the powerful of his day want him stopped, even if that requires his death. However, Jesus rejects a life lived in fear and instead lives—and dies—for the reign of God.

Orlando Espín has noted that Jesus "bet his life on his hope… that God had begun to transform this world into a new human reality built on compassion," a hope that is vindicated when God raises Jesus from the dead.[2] God confirms that Jesus is right to have given his life in love and hope for God's reign. Jesus' resurrection also stands as a reminder of the divine promise that God's reign will one day come in full for all, including the dead. The powerful of this world will not have the final say on the meaning of history or the value of the lives of the poor and marginalized, the "disposable" ones who are so often the victims of those who dominate and rule in history.

Christians are called to continue this tradition, remembering Jesus by following his example and betting their own lives, as Jesus did, on the hope for God's reign. Yet the New Testament also instructs Christians to remember Jesus in the sharing of the sacred bread and wine through which they become Christ's body for the world. As described in the Gospel of Luke, at his final meal with his disciples in celebration of the Passover, Jesus shared bread and wine and commanded his disciples to "do this in remembrance of me" (Luke 22:19; 1 Cor 11:23–25).

This eucharistic sharing of blessed bread and wine is a thanksgiving (*eucharistia* in Greek) for what God has done for the world in and through Jesus. Representing—making present again—Jesus' gift of himself and his life, the Eucharist forms Christians collectively to be Christ's Body, so that this expression of gratitude to God nourishes a community that continues Jesus' work of bringing God's reign to all.

Jesus' request that his followers remember him "as often as they do this" could also be understood as commanding his disciples to remember Jesus whenever they have food and drink. Jesus surely intended his disciples to continue his practice of open table fellowship so that, whenever they eat, they eat as Jesus did: building community with the people that society rejects as disposable and disreputable, those with whom social conventions discourage us from eating.

In any case, it would be difficult to claim that Jesus is remembered rightly when bread and wine are enjoyed without concern for those who lack sufficient food as well as the other material and immaterial resources of community life. As St. Paul reminded the Corinthians, the Lord's Supper is not properly celebrated amid practices of exclusion and hierarchy (see 1 Cor 11:20–22).

Christian memory is thus a practical memory, a tradition in which Jesus' commitment to God's inclusive reign of justice and harmony is remembered in actions—and not merely in words. This communal tradition, this Christian memory-in-action, is shaped and deepened by the biblical texts that past generations collected, preserved, and passed down (often with great difficulty) through millennia. These various and complex writings, from different contexts and with diverse perspectives, continue to challenge and to enrich the Christian community and its tradition of active (and subversive) hope in the God of our Jewish and Christian forbears.

CHRISTIAN TRADITION: THE COMMUNION OF SAINTS

Go into a church with stained glass windows along the side walls, and you may find that those windows depict holy people from the Bible or from Christian history. In addition to scenes from the life of Jesus, there might be representations of the disciples who courageously spread the gospel—saints like St. Peter and St. Paul or St. Mary Magdalene and the other women who were the first witnesses of the resurrection. There may also be a portrayal of the patron saint of the church, perhaps St. Patrick or St. Brigid, who nurtured the Christian faith in Ireland. Of course, depictions of Mary, the mother of Jesus and of the Christian community (according to a traditional interpretation of the Gospel of John) is especially common.[3]

If you stay to join a congregation gathered for worship in this space, you will then find yourself praying surrounded by what the Letter to the Hebrews calls a "cloud of witnesses" (Heb 12:1–2). It is as though the living in the pews and the dead pictured along the walls are joined together in one community worshipping God.

This is—and is intended to be—a visual experience of the dynamic community that has sustained and passed on Christian faith (including the Bible) through the centuries. This community of Christians came to be described in the early church as the "communion of saints," and is affirmed as an article of faith in the Apostles' Creed, an ancient statement of Christian belief that has been recited for over 1,500 years. The fact that the Apostles' Creed mentions the communion of saints reminds us that past generations have considered this a significant part of Christian faith.

Yet today this doctrine (or official teaching) about the communion of saints is seldom given much attention, and it is often misunderstood, if it is considered at all. Some people assume that "saints" are only people who have died, the holy ones in heaven, so that the communion of saints would not include those of us still living.

This mistaken understanding may be especially common among Catholics who know that Catholic Church authorities officially give the title of "saint" only to those who have died and whose lives are therefore complete. But in fact everyone who is in a state of friendship with God or, in traditional and more technical language, a state of sanctifying grace, is properly called a saint, even if not one officially recognized by church authorities.

The communion of saints thus refers to the profound union of all in God, whether living or dead. All Christians, past and present, are joined in a relationship of mutuality, which is why many Christians pray for the dead and ask the dead to pray for them. Moreover, as the union of all in God, the communion of saints is not oriented only to the past and the dead but also to the future and those yet to come. As long as history continues, this community is incomplete.

Recognizing this communion, or deep fellowship, among the living and the dead reminds us that we are part of an ongoing tradition, a community through time with resources beyond those of the finite and fallible present. Generations of wise and holy Christians have contributed profound insights and inspiring forms of Christian witness: consider St. Francis of Assisi's simple poverty and love of nature, St. Catherine of Siena's prayerful devotion to mysticism along with activism on behalf of her community, and Blessed Oscar Romero's heroic commitment to the poor of El Salvador, to mention just a few of the compelling examples of Christian holiness honored by the church. Indeed, we can be Christians today only because past Christians have passed this faith down to us. It follows then that those of us who value this heritage have a responsibility, in turn, to pass on to future generations what we have received.

But Christian faith is not (and should not be!) handed on as something static or unchanging. To be a member of the communion of saints is to be part of a living and growing tradition. Faithful women and men throughout Christian history have enriched our understanding of the witness of the Bible and the early disciples. As generations of Christians explore the meaning of Christianity in their specific contexts, we learn more of what it means to follow Jesus and to resist the many forms of exclusion and injustice in this broken world. Christian hope has been deepened by the contributions of multitudes of faithful people who have lived their profound commitment to the reign of God at different times and in different ways. So too must each new generation contribute its own best insights to further develop this tradition.

It is important to be clear that passing on this faith is not primarily about teaching statements of beliefs. Being a Christian is not a matter of merely affirming a collection of ideas to be thought— whether these ideas come from the Bible or from later church interpretations (such as the Apostles' Creed). Christian faith is best understood as a hope to be lived in love of God and of God's creation, a practice of love that resists the injustice and exclusion of the current world.

Doctrines have their place, of course. They remind us of the depth of the Christian tradition and its resources for empowering commitment to God's reign. Christians throughout the centuries have faced profound questions about the meaning of Christianity, and have worked together to develop explanations that the broader community recognizes as appropriate statements of their common faith. These clarifications, or doctrines, are valuable aids to the collective Christian memory. At their best, doctrines express the wisdom achieved by past generations, and call attention to aspects of Christian experience that might otherwise be overlooked or forgotten in a particular time.

The belief in the communion of saints is one such doctrine that deserves to be remembered not only in thought but also in practice. In a culture that so easily forgets the dead and assumes that only the living matter, the doctrine of the communion of saints is a reminder that those who have died remain beloved members of the Christian community. Christian hope includes a hope that these dead will be resurrected into the awaited—and longed for—fullness of God's reign.

The dead we are asked to remember include, of course, the officially acknowledged saints, those extraordinary people whose lives provide models of holiness that inspire and guide our efforts to live Christian discipleship in our time. But we must also, and perhaps especially, remember our own dead, those known only to God and to a small number of friends and family. After all, when we forget the dead, when they no longer matter to us, then how can we—who will soon join the dead sustain a sense of the value of our own brief lives?[4]

The doctrine of the communion of saints reminds Christians that we are joined together in a bond that does not end at death. The point of remembering the saints is not to elevate past holy people into minor deities, but to recognize that the church is a dynamic community that is not limited by time or space—it is a fellowship that includes all who live in God's love, whether in heaven or on earth.

It is this communion that has borne and continues to bear a tradition of hope in a compassionate God, the hope that Jesus inherited from his Jewish ancestors and the hope that he gave his life to. All are invited to join this communion and to continue to witness through their lives to this enduring hope for God's reign of love and inclusive justice.

LIVING HOPE

What difference would it make if Christians in the United States were to live more intentionally as members of this communion of saints, steeped in its tradition of subversive hope for everyone, including the dead and those yet to come?

Such a community, sharing a hope for the union of all in God, is obviously a countercultural challenge to society's current emphasis on individualism and consumerism. Participating in an ongoing tradition shifts the focus from temporary pleasures to valuing relationships and projects larger than one's self and one's immediate concerns. As members of a community united by a tradition of hope for God's reign, Christians are empowered to struggle—in hope—for compassionate inclusion and justice in society.

Learning to value tradition does not devalue the person (as I once thought), but rather underscores the difference that each life can make. People who know their debt to the past more easily recognize their obligation to the future. In particular, those who treasure the heritage of hope in God's compassion feel a responsibility to take part in transmitting this faith to future generations.

Being a member of a tradition, especially one that emphasizes communion with those who have died, also reminds us that life has a significance beyond death, and even beyond what is achieved and passed on to future generations. It is not only the "successful" whose lives matter, but all people, including those many victims of injustice and marginalization who have been prevented from making their full contribution to history. The dead, with their unrealized hopes and dreams, remain significant—to God, of course, but also to the community that remembers and continues to hope for them.

The memory of Jesus' resurrection thus stands as a promise for all who have died. The God who raised Jesus inspires hope that this same God can yet make right the pain and the loss, the unjust destruction of cherished hopes and dreams, even for the dead. As members of a community that has continued through centuries to anticipate God's coming reign, Christians await the future vindication of all who have been crushed by history.

However much tradition emphasizes the contributions of the past, then, tradition is by no means solely (or even primarily) backward looking. To the contrary, being part of a community through time orients one toward the future. This future-directedness is especially needed now, with human actions altering the conditions of life on this planet. The burning of fossil fuels for the past 150 years is causing the earth's climate to change so radically that the future of human civilization is at stake, along with the biodiversity of this planet. We cannot afford to continue ignoring the ecological impact of our consumerism.

Climate change is the greatest challenge humanity currently faces, and how we respond now will affect future generations. Humanity must decide, together and soon, whether we will persist with habits of consumption that destroy the natural balance that sustains all life on earth, or whether we will instead develop an economy that uses resources sustainably and for the good of all—including future generations.

The biblical traditions recognize a moral obligation to avoid greed (one of the seven deadly sins!) and to act with charity, sharing any abundance with those who are without essentials. Surely, this responsibility to avoid waste and to share with those in need includes an obligation not to waste the resources that will be needed by future generations. The subversive hope in God's reign of harmony orients us to face the future with a hope for all, a future that encompasses the dead, those not yet born, and as Pope Francis has recently reminded us, all of creation (*Laudato Si'*, esp. nos. 99–100).

Transforming our global economy into one of sustainability rather than excess and waste is a huge, and hugely important, task. It will require all of the resources we can muster, including the communal wisdom of traditions that broaden our perspectives and remind us of our debt to the past and our responsibility to the future.

The importance of being part of a community that embraces a living tradition of memory and hope was particularly well expressed by the noted American theologian Reinhold Niebuhr. Though he lived before climate change was a recognized problem, he knew that all struggles for a better world require a long perspective and communal effort:

> Nothing that is worth doing can be achieved in our life-time; therefore, we must be saved by hope. Nothing that is true or beautiful or good makes complete sense in any immediate context of history; therefore, we must be saved by faith. Nothing we do, however virtuous, can be accomplished alone; therefore we must be saved by love.[5]

Chapter 7

A PUBLIC FAITH IN A PLURALISTIC SOCIETY

IN 1964, IN THE MIDST of the Civil Rights Movement, the Rev. Jerry Falwell denounced religious leaders (such as the Rev. Martin Luther King Jr.) for inserting Christianity into politics. Drawing on ideas common in his Independent Baptist community, Falwell maintained that Christian faith is concerned only with transforming individual souls and so has no place in politics. Bringing religion into political matters such as the fight for equality for African Americans was a distraction from the true, spiritual, purpose of Christianity, Falwell argued.[1]

Fifteen years later, in 1979, Falwell founded the Moral Majority with the express purpose of doing what he had earlier condemned: Falwell organized evangelical Christians into a powerful political force in the United States. The Moral Majority movement worked to make U.S. laws consistent with the beliefs of conservative Christians, supported the candidacy of Ronald Reagan for president, and influenced the official platform of the Republican Party.

This unusually clear reversal—from being utterly opposed to religion in politics to being one of the most successful leaders of a Christian political organization—reminds us of the complexity of including religion in public life, particularly in a pluralistic society.

DIVINE HARMONY

After all, Falwell is hardly alone in shifting his position. Many liberal Christians who applauded the religious rhetoric of the Civil Rights Movement later decried the Moral Majority's efforts to pass laws based on their religious beliefs.

Something more than mere political opportunism is going on here. People often appreciate the support religion gives to their political issues, but nevertheless feel a fundamental discomfort—or at least confusion—about the extent to which religion ought to be involved in political debates. Few can give a coherent account of when and how religion is appropriately political, especially since, as Falwell noted in his early sermon against religious politics, religion can be deeply divisive. How can we hold together a religiously diverse society if our religious differences become part of our political disagreements?

This question goes to the heart of this book's project of defending inclusive, diverse communities based on the Christian ideal of persons-in-community. If Christian faith is the motivation for constructing these communities that unite people in their differences, how can such communities be truly inclusive of people of other religions? Isn't this a contradiction, particularly given religion's tendencies to divide people, often violently?

This new century provides ample evidence of religion as a socially divisive force. Massacres in the Middle East, Africa, and even Europe are justified on religious grounds. Tensions between Hindus and Muslims in India break out in mob violence, and the Muslim Rohingya are forced to live in concentration camps in the predominantly Buddhist Myanmar.

The attempt to achieve peace by keeping religion out of politics in the secular West is understandable in the face of religious violence. But this privatization of religion has itself become a source of division. The prohibition of the hijab (Muslim head scarf) in French schools is the cause of considerable societal conflict, as is the U.S. law requiring employers to include birth control in health insurance regardless of whether the religious beliefs of the employers oppose birth control. More broadly, many argue that secularism is not truly neutral, but rather privileges atheism over any and all religious beliefs.

In the midst of these debates about the public role of religion, three major approaches have emerged. First, there is still considerable support for the long-standing Western tendency to privatize religion, treating religion as a matter of personal practice that should be kept out of politics. The early (1960s) Jerry Falwell is not alone in understanding Christianity to be concerned only with one's individual soul and not with political issues. A second model has emerged that supports an explicit public acknowledgment of the religion or religious values deemed essential to hold society together, as argued by the later Falwell's Moral Majority movement. A third option advocates the sectarian withdrawal of religious believers to form their own distinct communities within the larger pluralistic state. The Amish or Old Order Mennonite communities throughout the Midwest, or even at times the Catholic Worker houses that personally welcome and care for the poor but eschew political engagement, are embodiments of this third approach.

Yet there are significant problems with each of these positions. None seems to allow for the inclusive, diverse societies consistent with the persons-in-community view advocated here, and none has so far become the basis for a new consensus on the role of religion in pluralistic societies.

Consider the privatization of religion, which until recently was largely unquestioned in American society. This approach remains attractive to many because, if religion is a private affair, then the religious diversity of the United States need not disrupt our public life. Religious beliefs would not influence political debates, and legislation should not address religious matters. Each adult could choose for him/herself whether to attend church, believe in God, or engage in practices such as divorce, drinking alcohol, dancing, or using birth control. As long as religious beliefs and practices are kept out of politics, then religious disagreements would not undermine the peace of the community.

Yet it is no longer clear that a consistent privatization of religion is possible. As society grows in complexity and diversity, it is difficult to create laws that do not infringe on someone's religious beliefs. As we have found in the United States, even governmental efforts to regulate hallucinogenic drugs or to protect health care consumers can lead to disputes over religious freedom.

A further debate has emerged over whether public neutrality on religion—if it were possible—would be desirable. Many argue that their religious faith informs all aspects of their lives, so that a rigorous separation of church and state prevents the full practice of their religion—they are required to check their faith at the door (so to speak) of their activity as citizens. Indeed, some contend that a neutral society compels all to act as atheists since it banishes reference to God from public institutions and political debates.

In fact, religious beliefs have been woven into the fabric of American public discourse since before the foundation of the United States. To be sure, the First Amendment to the U.S. Constitution prohibits the government from establishing any religion. Yet the Declaration of Independence referred to a Creator as the source of human rights, nineteenth-century arguments both for and against slavery appealed to God's will, and the Reverend Dr. Martin Luther King Jr. frequently cited biblical passages to inspire support for the Civil Rights Movement in the twentieth century, to mention just a few examples.

With the privatization of religion no longer the obvious solution, the alternative of an explicit public role for religion is gaining adherents. In this "religious establishment" option, religious principles would be recognized as the basis of social unity and especially of a country's laws.

There are various forms of this approach, with real distinctions between them. The explicit role of Islamic clerics in determining the laws of Iran is not the same as the claim that the United

States is implicitly a "Christian" nation, with its laws and social institutions conforming to general Christian principles. Yet these approaches share a commitment to replacing the privatization of religion with a public role for particular religious beliefs. All who want to participate in the political process or to take part in public institutions would have to accept that their political activities must be consistent with the dominant religion, even if they might have the freedom in private to subscribe to another religion (or to reject religion altogether).

But this religious establishment—whether explicit or implicit—is seriously problematic in a religiously pluralistic modern society. When a polity is organized according to the principles of one religion, all those who do not share the beliefs of that religion risk being marginalized as citizens, just as believers are marginalized when society insists that no religion will be allowed to influence politics. Moreover, this insistence on religious conformity in public is far from the celebration of diversity envisioned by the Christian ideal of persons-in-community that has been defended above.

Those who support some version of sectarianism (our third option) generally agree with advocates of religious establishment that society should be organized according to the tenets of their religion. However, sectarians have given up on the project of transforming the larger society in accord with their beliefs. Unable or perhaps simply unwilling to attain the power necessary to establish their religion, they seek to form a distinct community within the larger society, and to live together in that community according to their shared religious beliefs.

When we think of the sectarian option, the Amish or the Old Order Mennonites mentioned previously usually come to mind. They do not participate in the political system and refuse to go to war; instead, they strive to live simply and in communities of mutual support that witness against the individualism and materialistic greed of American society. But there are other forms of sectarianism. Megachurches that have expanded their campuses to provide food and entertainment to keep their members together at church as much as possible are certainly moving in the sectarian direction. So are the small groups of families that support each other in homeschooling and in other alternatives to participation in the institutions of what they consider a decadent society.

Even while those who advocate the sectarian option refuse direct action to change the larger society, sectarians may well hope that their withdrawal is itself a means of social transformation. After all, the manifestly different form of life that sets the sect apart from others can be an effective form of witness. Indeed, it is arguable that a distinct, alternative society-within-a-society of fully committed members is an important way for religious believers to model a truly harmonious community and, by implication, to show the world how misguided the rest of society is.

The sectarian option can thus provide a valuable witness of (some) religious values, but like the other two options, sectarianism precludes the engagement with diversity that is integral to the Christian understanding of persons-in-community. The privatization option also, of course, prevents public engagement with diverse religious beliefs insofar as it keeps religious differences confined to the private realm. With religious establishment, the religious positions relevant to public life have already been determined, so here too there is little room for public discussion of religious alternatives (which would destabilize society's religious consensus). The sectarian model goes even further, refusing in principle to build community and to seek common ground with those outside of the sect of committed believers.

It is no simple thing to figure out how religious people might bring their different beliefs into a mutually enriching public exchange. What could be more fraught than to engage political differences that embody our most sacred beliefs? Negotiating religious diversity remains a major challenge, and progress seems unlikely based on the currently dominant options of privatization, religious establishment, and sectarianism. Dare we hope that there might be a fourth option?

THE BIBLE: THEOCRACY, ACCOMMODATION, OR RESISTANCE?

Neither the Hebrew Bible nor the New Testament provides clear instructions about the public role of religion appropriate to today's diverse societies. After all, these ancient texts arose in very different circumstances from those of our modern pluralistic democracies. For one thing, the ancient world generally took for granted that what we call religion was part of what united a society—it is not at all clear that they understood *religion* to be a distinct category of behavior or activity. It should also be remembered that the Jews were often under foreign rule, including during the time of Jesus and the beginning of Christianity. During these periods, the ancient Jews did not have the final say on the laws they were governed by, even if their imperial conquerors made some concessions to Jewish culture and beliefs.

Rather than seeking a blueprint from the Bible for how to manage religious diversity in modern societies, we would be better off looking to general biblical themes for inspiration about how best to construct communities today. This, as we'll see later, is the approach taken in official Catholic teachings on the role of religion in the modern world.

Still, it cannot be denied that much of the Hebrew Bible supports a theocratic approach to governance, that is, the idea that society should be ruled by God's will, usually as interpreted by religious authorities. The law codes in the Torah (or Pentateuch, the first five books of the Bible) present a set of rules that are held as divinely given and as governing all aspects of life: political, economic, cultic, and familial. The biblical prophets provide further support for this form of religious establishment, since the prophets are understood as sent by God to correct rulers who deviate from the just rule specified in the Mosaic covenant.

Jesus' preaching of the reign (or kingdom) of God in the New Testament can also be invoked as evidence that the Bible supports theocratic government. The Gospels portray Jesus as focusing his message on the idea that the reign of God—where God's will is done by all—is coming now (or soon) to earth. It would seem that there could scarcely be a clearer support for Christian theocracy.

However, these same texts can also be used (along with the Book of Revelation) to defend sectarianism. If there are not enough committed believers to make the ideal of government according to God's rule a reality, then perhaps Christians should withdraw into intentional communities where they can at least govern themselves according to God's will. Such countercultural Christian communities find support in the Book of Revelation, which encourages the churches of Asia Minor to hunker down, refuse to participate in the evils of the (then) ruling Roman emperor, and await divine vindication.

And yet, other important biblical passages can be interpreted as defending religious privatization, suggesting that religious belief is a matter of personal spirituality that should not influence government or public life.

In the Hebrew Bible (or Christian Old Testament), two beloved stories describe faithful Hebrews who not only cooperate with but actually work for governments that do not recognize the Hebrew God or God's laws. The Book of Genesis includes the story of Joseph, who serves the Pharaoh and indeed is second only to the Pharaoh in governing Egypt. Even though the Pharaoh is considered divine and plays an integral role in the ancient Egyptians polytheistic religious system, nevertheless God provides Joseph with foreknowledge of the coming famine—knowledge that enriches the Pharaoh and ensures Joseph's success.

Similarly, the Book of Daniel relates the story of the heroic Daniel who, in exile, is called to serve the Babylonian Empire that had destroyed the Temple and removed the Jews from their land.

Yet, even though the Babylonian kings are condemned and eventually punished for their hubris and sacrilege, Daniel is portrayed as serving these kings honestly and without compromising his religious faith. He maintains his personal religious practices of "kosher" eating habits and daily prayers, even when threatened with death. His fidelity is rewarded with God's protection in the lion's den.

This story certainly suggests that, as long as one resists any laws that infringe on religious practice, it is acceptable to cooperate with governments that do not recognize God or God's revealed laws.

It is worth noting that there is no religious relativism here. Clearly, the God of Israel is understood to be the one true God, and the moral of the story of Daniel is that Jews should remain faithful to God even at the risk of their lives. Nevertheless, both Joseph and Daniel are depicted as faithful Hebrew men whose religion is a largely personal affair that does not prevent them from serving a government that fails to recognize God. Problems arise for Daniel only when the king is persuaded to make a law against private prayer.

There are two New Testament teachings of Jesus that are also invoked to support religious privatization. In the Gospel of John (18:36), Jesus declares that his kingdom is not "from this world," while in the Synoptic Gospels, Jesus tells the Pharisees they should "give therefore to the emperor the things that are the emperor's, and to God the things that are God's" (see Matt 22:21; Mark 12:17; Luke 20:25). These passages are often interpreted as clarifying that political issues are not properly spiritual concerns. Jesus, many conclude, is here declaring that his mission is a religious one and, as such, does not affect politics.

Yet biblical scholars have challenged the idea that these passages demonstrate that God's reign is an apolitical matter without relevance for this-worldly politics. After all, Jesus also taught his followers to pray, "Your kingdom come. / Your will be done, on earth as it is in heaven" (Matt 6:10). The statement that Jesus' kingdom is not "from this world" might be better understood, then, as asserting that Jesus' kingdom is not built on the coercion and domination that all political rule in this world relies upon. After all, throughout the Gospel of John, to be from or of this world is to be blind to spiritual truth. One can be in this world, as Jesus and his followers are, without sharing in the corruption and violence, the spiritual blindness, of this world.

It is also doubtful that Jesus' response to the question about paying taxes is properly interpreted as recognizing a division between those things that belong to rulers (i.e., political and social issues that affect this world) and those things that belong to God (e.g., spiritual and religious matters of relevance to one's afterlife). Jesus agrees with the Hebrew Bible that we are to love God with our whole hearts, souls, minds, and strength (see Mark 12:30; Matt 22:37; Luke 10:27; Deut 6:5). How then could there be an area of our lives that God does not rule?

Many have noted that Jesus was cleverly escaping a trap the Pharisees had laid for him. By producing a coin with the emperor's image on it, the men interrogating Jesus reveal that they themselves had violated the religious law against images. Jesus' point may be that we cannot avoid entanglement with governing authorities, and so we should not refuse them their due cooperation.

Perhaps the further message here is that money itself is part of the corruption, the domination and oppression, inherent in the politics of this world. Jesus may be reminding his followers that he calls them to a different set of values, and especially to an ethics of mutual care in which status has no place. This Christian ethic would be an alternative not only to collaboration with Rome, but also to the nationalism that threatens to become simply one more system of domination.

The letters of St. Paul are another biblical source cited in favor of religious privatization. In Romans 13:1, St. Paul declares that all should obey their rulers since, he asserts, all political authority comes from God—even, apparently, the authority of the pagan Roman emperors. St. Paul further advises Christians in 1 Thessalonians to live quietly, maintaining their good reputation with non-Christians (4:10–12). Insisting that Christians should accept the status quo of pagan imperial rule, St. Paul may seem to be suggesting that Christian faith is a personal matter not concerned with transforming society.

Yet it should be kept in mind that St. Paul expects the return of Jesus in his lifetime (see 1 Thess 4:15–17). Though St. Paul clearly does not advocate a Christian political revolution, he does assume all will be set right when Jesus returns in power. Rather than failing to appreciate the socially transformative implications of Christian belief, perhaps St. Paul is merely convinced that Jesus will soon change everything far beyond any human capacity to do so. And, of course, one must take into account the limited ability of Christians, a small and somewhat persecuted minority at this time, to effect social change. St. Paul may be better interpreted as politically pragmatic (given the circumstances of his time) rather than as advocating a private or apolitical faith.

Attention to the Bible thus demonstrates that, even when read carefully and with attention to context, the Bible can be cited in support of all three of the common options today: religious establishment, sectarianism, and privatization. To be sure, we must attend to a few consistent and pervasive themes. These include that the biblical God is deeply concerned with justice in society, but also (at least in the New Testament) that God promises a life of harmony beyond what can be achieved in this world. Nevertheless, the Bible leaves us with considerable latitude to work out what a faithful Christian politics requires at any particular time. We find here no definitive answer to our contemporary problem of determining the proper political role of religion, particularly in a modern pluralistic society.

CHURCH TRADITION: RELIGIOUS FREEDOM WITHOUT PRIVATIZATION

The issues posed by a religious diverse polity are relatively new in the long history of the Christian tradition. Christianity began under the pagan government of the Roman Empire. In these early years, Christian attention to politics was largely concerned with the problem of surviving without compromising Christian beliefs (especially since Christians resisted idol worship, including the often-necessary sacrifices to the emperor). After the conversion of Emperor Constantine in the early fourth century, this situation changed dramatically, and Christianity became the preferred and then the official religion of the empire that had once persecuted it.

This official status for Christianity was the predominant arrangement for the following (roughly) 1,500 years of Christian history. During this time, it was taken for granted that Christianity would be publicly recognized and supported by the political rulers. Of course, a distinction between political and religious powers was maintained—Pope Gelasius in the fifth century famously invoked the metaphor of "two swords" to represent the two authorities, religious and political, that he believed should cooperate in ruling society. It was assumed that society should be united religiously as well as politically, with both authorities working together for the good of the social order.

This assumption of religious and political unity was questioned in the sixteenth century by the more radical elements of the Protestant Reformation. The early Reformers (Martin Luther, Ulrich Zwingli, and John Calvin) continued to envision a religiously united society, though they wanted political leaders to support Protestant, rather than Catholic, Christianity. However, the more radical reformers, especially the Anabaptists, who sought a purer and more radical Christian witness, challenged the continuing union of church and state. Studying the New Testament stories of the early church, these proponents of the Radical Reformation discovered a church with a demanding communal life and a religious rigor beyond what is possible when church membership is determined, not by grace received in faith, but simply by being born into a particular society. They concluded that a countercultural faith community that refuses to compromise its commitment to the teachings of Christ requires a deep and personal faith from its members.

Thus began a significant modern Christian position advocating the separation of church and state. John Howard Yoder, a twentieth-century Mennonite theologian, developed an influential contemporary version of this approach, condemning the "Constantinian shift" in which church and state publicly support each other. He argued that Christians should refuse to participate in the power politics of the state so that the church might better witness to the alternative politics of the kingdom of God, which, he insisted, requires a pacifist refusal of all war. When Christianity became the ruling religion, Yoder maintained, the church conceded its proper mission of living the radical ethics taught by Jesus. Instead, Christians adapted their faith to what were assumed to be the practical requirements of power and rule in this world.[2]

Mainstream Protestants have largely rejected this Anabaptist model of the church as a sectarian countercultural community. Nevertheless, during the colonial era in the United States, a growing emphasis on personal religious commitment, along with the Enlightenment defense of liberty of conscience, increased support for religious disestablishment. Of course, there was also the practical impossibility of declaring an official common faith for colonies settled by members of different Christian denominations. This set the context for the United States to pioneer a modern approach to religious liberty, refusing the establishment of religion and promising freedom of religious practice. A country could be governed, the founders believed, without a common religion.

Religious freedom has since come to be widely accepted as a basic human right. Indeed, the United Nations General Assembly listed religious freedom among the human rights affirmed in its 1948 "Universal Declaration of Human Rights." Even though this declaration includes the right to express one's beliefs publicly, much of Western society has presumed that religion is ultimately a private matter, irrelevant to public life.[3] Because religion is commonly understood to be irrelevant to the organization of society, many have concluded that government has no need to encourage or discourage the religious beliefs of its citizenry.

It was this religious privatization, along with the often implied religious indifferentism (the idea that what one believes doesn't really matter), that the official Catholic Church could not accept. So Catholic Church leaders continued until the mid-twentieth century to insist that the preferred political arrangement is an official Catholic state, with government support for Catholicism and suppression of any public teaching of other religious views. Indeed, as late as 1955, the American Jesuit priest and scholar John Courtney Murray was "silenced"—that is, he was ordered not to publish further arguments in support of the U.S. model of religious freedom. The Catholic Church only officially approved of religious liberty when the bishops at the Second Vatican Council, after much debate, issued its Declaration on Religious Freedom, more commonly known as *Dignitatis Humanae* in 1965 (nearly two decades after religious freedom had been overwhelmingly endorsed by the United Nations).[4]

Troubling as it is that the Catholic authorities were so late to accept religious liberty, it is just this difficulty that makes Vatican II's defense of religious freedom so instructive today. Emphasizing the social nature of the person, Catholic Christianity has consistently rejected the idea that religion is an individual, private matter, irrelevant to the larger society. The contribution of *Dignitatis Humanae* is that it sets forth a thoroughly Christian alternative to religious establishment that also clearly refuses privatization and sectarian withdrawal.

Dignitatis Humanae begins its endorsement of religious freedom with an affirmation of personal judgment and of responsible freedom as integral to the dignity of the person. Acknowledging that the Bible does not affirm religious liberty "in so many words," the document nevertheless argues that Scripture reveals that God intends human beings to be free to accept or to reject God's offer of love. That God gave humanity this freedom is evident in the stories of Genesis and in God's relationship with his chosen people throughout the Hebrew Bible, as well as in the New Testament accounts of Jesus' refusal to coerce faith. Since God respects human freedom in matters of religion, so too should political authorities (and indeed all people).

This endorsement of religious freedom in society is not, however, to be understood as "religious indifferentism," or what we might today call "relativism." *Dignitatis Humanae* maintains that there is indeed religious truth (even if we must acknowledge that no human being has or can have the full truth). Further, all people have a duty to seek the truth and to embrace it when found. Besides, no one can really be coerced into accepting the truth, though people can and often do respond to force by pretending to agree. As *Dignitatis Humanae* notes, "The truth cannot impose itself except by virtue of its own truth, as it makes its entrance into the mind at once quietly and with power" (no. 1).

Moreover, the human search for truth as described in *Dignitatis Humanae* is a communal endeavor. As persons-in-community, we come to greater truth through dialogue with others, as we share insights and evaluate perspectives. Indeed, as social beings who learn from each other, our duty to the truth includes a duty to share our insights with one another. Hence, *Dignitatis Humanae* envisions a vigorous and free public conversation: religious freedom is to be granted not because religion doesn't matter, but rather because the truth about religious questions matters so much that we must join our resources and energies in a common effort to attain greater truth.

Dignitatis Humanae further affirms the importance of including religion in the public conversation—in opposition to religious privatization—by noting that religion has implications for politics and the public order. It is part of religious freedom as understood in this document that "religious communities should not be prohibited from undertaking to show the special value of their doctrine in what concerns the organization of society" (no. 4). This document thus affirms the traditional Catholic position that religious beliefs are relevant to public life, justice, and the common good.

But we might then wonder whether *Dignitatis Humanae* is in fact presenting a consistent position. How can this document coherently maintain that religious beliefs should influence decisions about the government of society and, at the same time, insist that people should be free from government interference in matters of religion? If religious beliefs are taken into account in the development of legislation, it would seem to follow that the resulting laws will fit with some religious beliefs but not with others. Faced with this situation, many have concluded that when religion is allowed into politics and government, religious freedom is compromised.

Dignitatis Humanae, however, contends that the resolution to this apparent impasse between establishment and privatization is to be found in dialogue and persuasion, especially insofar as all people have a right to participate democratically in determining their own government. Religious values should affect politics not by government mandate, but by contributing to a consensus arising from public debate in the search for truth.

Further, when religious values seek to influence law, the focus must be on the purposes proper to the state—the public order, justice, and the common good of society (and ultimately of the world). After all, if we legislate all morality, we overtax the resources of government and limit the realm of human freedom. People cannot make truly moral choices when coerced by threat of punishment. So it is crucial to ensure that legislation only addresses matters appropriate to the limited purposes of the state.

Of course, this leaves unresolved the question of what the purposes of the state should be. More specifically, how are we to define the public order, justice, and the common good? This is an issue open to debate, and one in which religious beliefs might well inform people's views. Surely, our deepest values influence how we understand what justice requires and what the common good is.

Fortunately, a political agreement about the goals of government does not depend on the (highly unlikely) achievement of complete agreement about religion. Instead, the Catholic tradition maintains that the principles of proper government, though often clarified by religion, can also be discerned through reason. The values that Christians should espouse in public life, and in particular what we need to flourish as persons-in-community, are in principle able to be recognized and affirmed by non-Christians, who may come to these same values through other religions or through reason alone. As Pope Francis reminds us in his encyclical on the environment, "The ethical principles capable of being apprehended by reason can always reappear in different guise and find expression in a variety of languages, including religious language" (*Laudato Si'* 199).

Dignitatis Humanae thus proposes public conversation as an alternative to religious privatization and religious establishment (or sectarianism). We do not have to choose between keeping our religious beliefs to ourselves, on the one hand, or ensuring that society is organized and governed according to an established religious perspective, on the other hand. Instead, we should engage in political discourse as a common search together for the truth, including the truth about the values that ought to direct our society. Understanding ourselves as persons-in-community, Christians should be especially devoted to persuading people to foster the inclusive, diverse communities in which the dignity of all persons is respected.

One more point should be noted here: religious freedom as described in *Dignitatis Humanae* is not—and cannot be—an absolute right that trumps all other rights. As important as religious freedom is, the government nevertheless has a responsibility to keep people from violating others' rights or disrupting the public order, even when religion is invoked as the motivation for such abuses (see *Dignitatis Humanae* 7). While governments should allow as much religious freedom as possible, there must, of course, be limits on what people are allowed to do in the name of religious freedom.

DIVINE HARMONY

RELIGIOUS DIVERSITY
WITHOUT DIVISION

In late December of 2015, a group of Somali terrorists ambushed a Kenyan bus of (mostly) women traveling near the Somali border. Such attacks are common in that area, and usually result in the massacre of the Christian travelers. In this case, however, the quick-thinking Muslim women loaned hijabs (head scarves) to the Christian women, and refused the terrorists' order to separate from them. In a courageous witness to community across religious lines, the Muslim women reportedly informed the terrorists that all present were Muslims, announcing, "If you want to kill us, then kill us. There are no Christians here." Thus stymied in their plans to identify and execute Christians, the terrorists left without killing anyone aboard the bus.[5]

The courage and solidarity shown by these Muslim women is impressive. They put their own lives on the line to save the lives of others. It's hard to imagine a better witness to the belief that we belong to one another than that of these Muslim women who, despite threats from armed men intent on murder, refused to abandon Christians to a certain death.

This incident is especially instructive because it occurred during a period of considerable religious conflict between Christians and Muslims. Terrorists are invoking extreme interpretations of Islam to justify mass killings of civilians, and many Christians respond with an Islamophobia that denigrates all members of this major world religion. The example of these Kenyan women reminds us that this spiral of increasing conflict and distrust is not inevitable. Religious diversity does not need to cause division, and hostility does not have to be met with greater hostility.

Not everyone has the occasion to risk his or her life as these brave Muslim women did, but all can contribute to building community across the many differences, including religious differences, currently dividing the human family. If religion is not to be an ongoing cause of conflict and polarization, religious diversity must be valued as a source of wisdom that can strengthen and enrich the life of the community. After all, the infinite God exceeds all human (and therefore finite) descriptions. And, the complexity of the modern world requires all of the best wisdom we have and the deepest insights we can muster about what makes for a worthwhile life and a stable community.

Seeking greater community amid human diversity is a special obligation for the Christian church, which, as we saw in chapter 5, is meant to be a sign and instrument of human unity in the world. Christians cannot fulfill their mission unless they are committed to building a more inclusive society, one in which people respectfully engage rather than marginalize others of different religions as well as classes, ethnicities, races, genders, and even ages. *Dignitatis Humanae* contributes to this task of fostering unity-in-diversity with its affirmation of a public conversation that includes religion in public debates about justice and the common good of society.

Above all, in and beyond any conversation, we need to witness—as the Muslim women on the Kenyan bus did—to a solidarity that resists polarization and segregation. Creating and sustaining relationships and even friendships with those who disagree with our deepest religious beliefs, or are otherwise different from us, is a more powerful and persuasive contribution to human unity than merely talking about the importance of unity amid diversity.

Some think that the word *religion* may have its origins in the Latin *re-ligare*, "to reconnect." This etymology is not certain, but there is no doubt that the challenge of religion today is to contribute to the unity of the human community, reconnecting the separated—even those separated religiously.

CONCLUSION

THE JOY OF THE GOSPEL

Whenever our interior life becomes caught up in its own interests and concerns, there is no longer room for others, no place for the poor. God's voice is no longer heard, the quiet joy of his love is no longer felt, and the desire to do good fades.

—Pope Francis, *Evangelii Gaudium*, no. 2

CHRISTIANITY (along with many other religions) understands humans as relational beings. People are created not to be isolated individuals but to realize our uniqueness in community, in loving harmony with all others in God. Our ultimate goal is not simply to be with God, as is often thought, but rather to be together with all of creation *within* God, enfolded into the loving life of a Triune God who longs to incorporate everything into the divine harmony. We find ourselves and our true joy not in isolation then, but in community bonds extending through time and space until all are finally gathered into a common life united by the love of God.

This realization that we are not truly separate individuals but rather are relational persons is deeply needed in the contemporary world. Consider the reality of globalization, bringing all of humanity together into a complex but integrated economic system. Humanity is increasingly interconnected, but on what terms? Will we come together in a globalization that enriches the common good and affirms the value of each—or will we relate to each other primarily as competitive individuals, with each seeking his or her immediate good at the expense of all others?

A global economy, for example, could foster international collaboration so that standards of living are raised and all share in the benefits of advances in medical care, agriculture, and technology. Indeed, there is good evidence that economic cooperation has significantly decreased the percentage of people in the world living in extreme poverty—and this is indeed cause for celebration.

But global economic forces can also redirect local economies so that they serve foreign markets to the detriment of the immediate community. Subsistence farming may be replaced with cash crops that leave people hungry when those crops lose their market value—or when the producers are not paid a living wage. Similarly, the threat of job relocation can suppress wages as workers compete globally to produce the most for the least pay. In fact, our global economy is such a massive and complex system that it is very difficult for consumers to learn about the conditions in which products are produced—and this invisibility allows horrific abuses, including slavery, to flourish.

The reality is that global capitalism as currently structured seeks ever-greater profits regardless of the impact on people, society, or the environment. This is presenting us with serious—and unprecedented—problems of inequality, environmental degradation, and mass human migration often due to economic and environmental pressures. Globalization thus threatens to cause great harm, especially through a complex economic system that no one quite controls, and from which only a minority fully benefit.

Problems of inequality, environmental degradation, and migration are not new, of course. But humanity has never grappled with these challenges on the scale we currently face. Economic systems, for example, have seldom benefitted all equally, but global capitalism is currently separating a rich minority with previously unimaginable luxuries from the majority of the human race, who struggle to attain the essentials of a secure and dignified life.

Human beings have depleted or polluted their environments throughout history, but we now have the capacity to change the conditions of all life on this planet. With the burning of fossil fuels causing total global climate change, humanity can do unprecedented damage to the natural processes that sustain human life as well as the lives of other species.

Likewise, there have always been refugees moving to escape drought, famine, and war. But we are currently experiencing such a large scale migration that people are dying in camps because the systems that aid refugees (especially in Europe) are overwhelmed by the numbers of desperate people forced to leave home in search of peace and security.

These are huge problems, and an ethos of competitive individualism does not help. Only if people recognize that our own well-being is tied to the flourishing of others—that is, only if we understand ourselves as persons-in-community—will we be able to rally the global cooperation necessary to solve these global problems. A competitive capitalism can make the ideal of persons-in-community seem unrealistic in the face of pressures to secure one's own good above all others, but in fact, nothing could be more pragmatic than the recognition that we are all in this together.

It has become obvious, for example, that no one country or community can absorb the multitudes who are currently refugees. This massive population shift requires a coordinated international response to ensure that the refugees are divided among enough countries that the welcoming communities are not overwhelmed. It will also take considerable international cooperation to resecure the home countries from which populations are fleeing. As current events demonstrate all too clearly, political or economic instability anywhere can affect the lives of people everywhere.

DIVINE HARMONY

The impending crisis of global climate change—perhaps the most important issue we face today—also clearly requires a global response. Without a shared commitment to reducing greenhouse gas emissions, the benefits of any decrease in fossil fuel use by some can easily be undone by others' overuse of these fuels. If each person or country seeks its own advantage, we cannot solve this crisis—and everyone will suffer the consequences (though the poor will probably suffer the most).

And, of course, a global economy will serve the common good only if enough people around the world are committed to working together to ensure that economic competition fosters the well-being of all rather than producing profits for the few. Collective action, involving much cooperation, is needed to develop national and international economic regulations that can channel the properly competitive elements of the economy toward the good of all.

A particular situation that begs for our attention—one where a persons-in-community approach is especially needed—is the current reality of "disposable" people. At home and abroad, many are without a place in society because they have no economic value. People who are not needed as producers (especially with the increasing mechanization of labor), and who are unable to participate as consumers, are too often discarded by societies that mirror the values of the economy.

Instead of valuing human life in terms of its economic worth, we need a clear recognition that all matter not because of what they can produce or consume but just because they exist—and are inherently a part of everyone else. No one is disposable: each person—indeed, every being—contributes to the richness and diversity of a world that shows forth God's goodness.

The capacity to appreciate each person as an irreplaceable part of the whole is also, of course, essential to one's own sense of self-worth. When we recognize that each person is an important part of the human community, then we implicitly affirm our own significance. Our value, like theirs, lies not in what we accomplish but in the fact that we are—and enrich others by simply being. Conversely, if we treat others as disposable when they are unable to make a measureable economic contribution, then we will come to see ourselves as also lacking in inherent value. And then we will strive to affirm our self-worth through piling up achievements in a brutal, competitive world, against that inevitable time when we too are no longer able to do enough to be significant.

Ultimately, of course, the confidence that we matter is, for Christians, grounded in God and not in ourselves, in our achievements, or even in the human community. It is God's love that creates and sustains each one of us, and God's love that offers us everlasting life together in loving community. Everyone has value because each person matters to God.

Because our hope is in God, we are (fortunately) not dependent on the fragile success of our human efforts. Looking to redemption beyond this world, we are freed from the idea that this-worldly success is the most important thing. The resulting freedom enables us to risk failure as we seek greater community even where we have the least likelihood of succeeding.

This hope for redemption beyond history should not, then, distract us from playing our part as best we can in our own time and place. Confidence that God can complete and preserve what we accomplish here gives our efforts great value. Indeed, all that we are and do in our lifetimes will continue to matter long after the human race and even the planet Earth have ceased to exist, if Christians are right in their hope that all will be preserved in and with God forever.

As Pope Francis recently reminded us, there is a liberating joy in this gospel message of God's redemptive love for each of us. The problems we confront are daunting, but we do not face them alone. God remains with us, forgiving our failures and, through the love and peace of the Holy Spirit, bringing us to the fullness of loving communion with God and one another.

NOTES

INTRODUCTION

1. Howard Thurman, *The Search for Common Ground: An Inquiry into the Basis of Man's Experience of Community* (New York: Harper & Row, 1971), xi.

CHAPTER 1. CALLED TO COMMUNITY

1. MarYam G. Hamedani, Hazel Rose Marcus, and Alyssa Fu, "In the Land of the Free, Interdependent Action Undermines Motivation," *Psychological Science* 24, no. 2 (February 2013): 189–96, at 189. Interestingly, these results were not found to apply to Asian Americans, a reminder of the cultural diversity in the United States.

2. Robert D. Putnam, *Bowling Alone: The Collapse and Revival of American Community* (New York: Simon and Schuster, 2001).

3. See, for example, the accusation that Jesus eats with tax collectors and sinners in Matt 9:10–11; Mark 2:15–17; and Luke 5:32.

4. This story is evidently important, as it is repeated throughout the Gospels (though the size of the crowd changes somewhat). The story can be found in Matt 14:13–21; 15:29–39; Mark 6:30–44; 8:1–10; Luke 9:10–17; and John 6:1–13.

5. See, for example, the two healing stories in Matt 8:1–10: the leper healed by touch and the centurion's servant healed without Jesus going to the house where he lay paralyzed and in pain.

6. In addition to 1 Cor 11, see 2 Cor 3:6 as well as the non-Pauline Letter to the Hebrews, chapters 8 and 9.

7. See especially, Pope John Paul II, On the Dignity and Vocation of Women, *Mulieris Dignitatem*, https://w2.vatican.va/content/john-paul-ii/en/

apost_letters/1988/documents/hf_jp-ii_apl_19880815_mulieris-dignitatem
.html, no. 7.

    8. Augustine, *The Confessions of St. Augustine*, trans. and with an introduction and notes by John K. Ryan (New York: Doubleday, 1960), 102, 255–56.

    9. Joseph Ratzinger (Pope Benedict XVI), "Communion: Eucharist—Fellowship—Mission," in his *Pilgrim Fellowship of Faith: The Church as Communion* (San Francisco: Ignatius Press, 2005), 60–90.

    10. Howard Thurman, Walter Earl Fluker, and Catherine Tumbler, *A Strange Freedom: The Best of Howard Thurman on Religious Experience and Public Life* (Boston: Beacon Press, 1998), esp. 254–55.

CHAPTER 2. EMBRACING INDIVIDUALITY AND DIVERSITY

    1. According to the U.S. Bureau of Labor statistics for 2015, 69.9 percent of women with children under the age of 18 participated in the workforce (i.e., were employed or looking for work outside the home). See http://www.bls.gov/news.release/famee.nr0.htm.

    2. These restrictions were later reversed. See the discussion at https://www.washingtonpost.com/blogs/she-the-people/wp/2014/08/13/pentagon-reverses-black-hairstyle-restrictions/?Post+generic=%3Ftid%3Dsm_twitter_washingtonpost.

    3. For the commands to fill the earth, see Gen 1:28 and 9:1.

    4. See especially the ecumenical statement on the church developed by the Faith and Order Commission of the World Council of Churches, *The Church: Towards a Common Vision*, Faith and Order Paper no. 214 (Geneva: WCC Publications, 2013), 17–19.

CHAPTER 3. REDEEMED–TOGETHER

    1. Walter Rauschenbusch, *Christianity and the Social Crisis in the Twenty-First Century: The Classic that Woke Up the Church* (New York: HarperCollins, 2007), 177–78.

    2. This question is explored in John Courtney Murray's classic essay, "Is It Basketweaving? The Question of Christianity and Human Values," in *We Hold These Truths: Catholic Reflections on the American Proposition* (Kansas City, MO: Sheed and Ward, 1960), 175–96.

    3. Pope Francis, On the Proclamation of the Gospel in Today's

Notes

World, *Evangelii Gaudium*, available at http://w2.vatican.va/content/
francesco/en/apost_exhortations/documents/papa-francesco_esortazione
-ap_20131124_evangelii-gaudium.html.

4. The Book of Ezekiel's vision of dead bones coming together is often assumed to be a description of individuals being raised from the dead, but this vision is actually a metaphor for the restoration of the people of Israel.

5. *Peaceable Kingdom* is the name of a series of paintings by the American Quaker Edward Hicks. These paintings include images of total harmony on earth, especially as described in the Book of Isaiah. In addition to Isa 2 and 11, see Mic 4:1–4.

6. The Book of Isaiah is thought to have at least two and probably three different authors, writing in different historical contexts (before the Babylonian exile, during the exile, and after the exile). See Christian E. Hauer and William A. Young, *An Introduction to the Bible: A Journey into Three Worlds* (Upper Saddle River, NJ: Prentice Hall, 2005), 137–40.

7. Although I have chosen to focus on the Synoptic Gospels here, the Gospel of John also has a thoroughly communal view of salvation as is evident in his description of the vine and branches in John 15:1–5.

8. See Richard A. Norris, Jr., trans. and ed., *The Christological Controversy* (Philadelphia: Fortress Press, 1980), esp. 1–31.

9. St. Gregory Nazianzus, "The First Letter to Cledonius the Presbyter" (Letter 101), in *On God and Christ: The Five Theological Orations and Two Letters to Cledonius*, trans. Lionel Wickham (Crestwood, NY: St. Vladimir's Seminary Press, 2002), 158.

10. Karl Rahner, "Christology within an Evolutionary View of the World," in *Theological Investigations*, vol. 5, *Later Writings*, trans. Karl H. Kruger (Baltimore: Helicon Press, 1966), 157–202.

11. For an especially clear discussion of Irenaeus's doctrine of recapitulation, see Adam Kotsko, "Irenaeus," in *The Politics of Redemption: The Social Logic of Salvation* (New York: T&T Clark International, 2010), 71–96.

12. See especially Pope Francis, On Care for Our Common Home, *Laudato Si'*, available at http://w2.vatican.va/content/francesco/en/encyclicals/documents/papa-francesco_20150524_enciclica-laudato-si.html. An excellent brief description of this interpretation of the Trinity is provided by Jürgen Moltman, *The Trinity and the Kingdom: The Doctrine of God* (Minneapolis: Fortress Press, 1991), 94–96.

13. Gustavo Gutiérrez, *A Theology of Liberation: History, Politics and Salvation* (Maryknoll, NY: Orbis Books, 1973), 153.

14. Second Vatican Council, The Pastoral Constitution on the Church in the Modern World, *Gaudium et Spes*, available at http://www .vatican.va/archive/hist_councils/ii_vatican_council/documents/vat-ii_cons _19651207_gaudium-et-spes_en.html.

CHAPTER 4. CHRISTIAN SPIRITUALITY

1. These experiences, including the events below, are recounted in Langdon Gilkey, *Shantung Compound: The Story of Men and Women under Pressure* (San Francisco: Harper & Row, 1960), especially 96–116 and 225–29.

2. One place this story is recounted is http://www.washingtonpost .com/wp-dyn/content/article/2006/11/21/AR2006112101801.html.

3. Compare Mary's Magnificat in Luke 1:46–55 with the prayer of Hannah in 1 Sam 2:1–10.

4. For a particularly clear discussion of this point, see Gustavo Gutiérrez, "The Ethics of the Kingdom," in *The God of Life*, trans. Matthew J. O'Connell (Maryknoll, NY: Orbis Books, 1991), 118–39.

5. Walter Rauschenbusch, *Christianity and the Social Crisis in the Twenty-First Century: The Classic that Woke Up the Church* (New York: HarperCollins Publishers, 2007), 213.

6. Walter Rauschenbusch, *Christianizing the Social Order* (New York: MacMillan Company, 1916), 44.

7. Rauschenbusch, *Christianity*, xxii.

8. Paul Tillich, *Love, Power, and Justice: Ontological Analyses and Ethical Applications* (Oxford: Oxford University Press, 1954), especially 57 and 71.

9. Pope Francis, On the Proclamation of the Gospel in Today's World, *Evangelii Gaudium*, available at http://w2.vatican.va/content/ francesco/en/apost_exhortations/documents/papa-francesco_esortazione -ap_20131124_evangelii-gaudium.html.

10. The phrase, "outsourcing our option for the poor," was suggested to me by a similar phrase used by Gary Arps, of St. Paul's Cathedral in San Diego. Mr. Arps frequently warned parishioners against outsourcing our social concerns.

11. See Marie Dennis, Renny Golden, Scott Wright, eds., *Oscar Romero: Reflections on His Life and Writings* (Maryknoll, NY: Orbis Books, 2000).

CHAPTER 5. GLOBAL COMMUNITY

1. The story and pictures can be found at http://www.nytimes
.com/2015/12/28/world/middleeast/syria-refugees-alan-aylan-kurdi.html?
_r=0.

2. Later experiences of exile and most notably the Babylonian captivity would have reminded the people of this earlier exile experience and reinforced their self-identity as foreigners.

3. Vatican Council II, Dogmatic Constitution on the Church, *Lumen Gentium*, available at http://www.vatican.va/archive/hist_councils/ii_vatican_council/documents/vat-ii_const_19641121_lumen-gentium_en.html.

4. World Council of Churches, *The Church: Towards a Common Vision*, Faith and Order Paper No. 214 (Geneva: World Council of Churches Publications, 2013), 5.

5. This ritual is profoundly captured in the film *One Border, One Body: Immigration & the Eucharist* (Notre Dame, IN: Gatekeeper Productions/University of Notre Dame, 2008).

CHAPTER 6. THE GIFT OF TRADITION

1. See similar statements in Exod 22:21; 23:21; Jer 22:3; Ezek 22:7; 22:29; Zech 7:10; and Mal 3:5.

2. Orlando Espín, *Idol and Grace: On Traditioning and Subversive Hope* (Maryknoll, NY: Orbis Books, 2014), 93, see also 6.

3. See John 19:26–27 for the story of Jesus placing his mother in the care of his "beloved disciple" and the disciple in the care of his mother.

4. For a development of this idea, see Johann Baptist Metz, *Faith in History and Society: Toward a Practical Fundamental Theology*, trans. J. Matthew Ashley (New York: Crossroad Publishing Company, 2007), esp. 82–84.

5. Reinhold Niebuhr and Andrew J. Bacevich, *Irony of American History* (Chicago: University of Chicago Press, 2008), 63.

CHAPTER 7. A PUBLIC FAITH IN A PLURALISTIC SOCIETY

1. See the discussion in Garry Wills, *Head and Heart: A History of Christianity in America* (New York: Penguin Books, 2007), 470, 481.

DIVINE HARMONY

2. See especially John Howard Yoder, *The Priestly Kingdom: Social Ethics as Gospel* (Notre Dame, IN: University of Notre Dame Press, 1985).

3. "The Universal Declaration of Human Rights" can be found in its entirety at http://www.un.org/en/universal-declaration-human-rights/index .html. See especially Article 18 on religious rights.

4. Vatican Council II, Declaration on Religious Freedom, *Dignitatis Humanae*, available at http://www.vatican.va/archive/hist_councils/ii _vatican_council/documents/vat-ii_decl_19651207_dignitatis-humanae_en .html.

5. A report of this incident can be found at http://www.cnn.com/ 2015/12/22/africa/kenya-bus-attack-al-shabaab-muslim-christians/.